You Came Into My Life

You Came Into My Life

Kenny Bernard

authorHOUSE®

AuthorHouse™
1663 Liberty Drive
Bloomington, IN 47403
www.authorhouse.com
Phone: 1-800-839-8640

First published by AuthorHouse   10/26/2011

ISBN: 978-1-4670-2350-4 (sc)
ISBN: 978-1-4670-2349-8 (ebk)

Printed in the United States of America

This book is printed on acid-free paper.

This book is written in memory of my beautiful wife Doreen who remains my guiding star to this very day. And my wonderful family who will always be my inspiration.

Thank you to them and to everyone who has helped me on my musical journey.

Acknowledgements

There are so many people I would like to thank, so many people who have helped me in music, and life, to get me to where I am today.

Most of all, I would like to thank my wonderful family, my children Dean and Marsha and my grandchildren Kyran and Jaden.

I would also like to thank everyone who ever performed with and in The Wranglers, memories I will always cherish.

While I cannot thank everyone who has helped me in my life—that would take a whole book in itself!—I would like to mention Kevin and Barbara Stannard, all my former colleagues at Jeyes, the Norfolk Terrier pub in Thetford, the George at Methwold, the Thetford British Legion, St Nicholas Hospice Care, staff at West Suffolk Hospital, the sports and social club in Thetford, Liz Richardson—a very good local singer who has helped me raise money for charity—Will Weaver and Peter Jay.

And to absolutely everyone else who has been part of the good times. I thank you all.

Kenny Bernard

Foreword

In a different life, with different choices, I could have achieved fame and fortune, had a gold disc hanging from a wall or an Oscar on my mantelpiece.

But I have never been one for regrets. You make your choices, you have your share of luck and you only remember the good times. And boy, were there some good times.

I have been very fortunate in my life to play at some of the greatest stages in England and to meet some truly amazing stars. I have equally had just as much enjoyment playing intimate gigs and local venues.

I sometimes hear these famous songs on the radio or see these great names being interviewed and wondered whether that could have been me.

But had that happened, where would I be and who would I have become? I doubt very much I would be writing this book today.

I have learnt from the bad times and loved having the good times.

I wouldn't have changed a thing.

Chapter One: The Streets Were Paved With Gold

My Mum was the most industrious woman you could meet. In a time when women were meant to play the dutiful housewife leaving the husband to earn the money, Mildred Bernard refused to play up to that particular stereotype.

She was a confident woman who was never afraid to stick up for what she believed in. This was especially true when it came to her family where she simply refused to settle for second best. My Dad, Clive, was more laidback, a typical Caribbean man you could say.

But Mum had fire in her belly. She ran the village post office when I was growing up. But to give us the best chance of a better life, she used the small office to also run a kindergarten behind the counter at the same time as handing out mail and selling stamps.

Born in 1921, she was bright and well-educated, having gone to the renowned Tranquillity Government Secondary School in Port of Spain, the capital of Trinidad. The newsreader, Sir Trevor McDonald, was also a former student, something that made me quite proud when I think about my dear Mum.

A drive for success was a feature of her life. She went on to become a successful hairdresser in San Fernando, one of the largest cities in Trinidad and Tobago, but even then something was yearning inside her. It was a yearning to make something even better for herself and her family.

I was born in Diego Martin, a town just north-west of the Port of Spain, on December 21st, 1943. I have one brother, Ansel, and one sister, Barbara, who were identical twins born three years after me.

Though never a qualified teacher, my Mum was great with children and would teach them, and us, some basic education. At that time, we lived next door to the local school which meant that when the time came for me to get my education, there was no excuse for me being late. The only problem was I never wanted to go in the first place.

I had a unique way of showing my dislike of school. First I bit the teacher within a few days of starting. And then it continued into my second week when I hatched what I thought was a great escape plan, a ruse to get out of going however close the school might be to my house.

After my Mum walked me the short distance, I waited for her to leave before sneaking back into our house next door and hiding behind the wardrobe for the whole day. I'm surprised I didn't venture out for snacks or just to explore, but no, there was me behind this wardrobe thinking I had got away with it. Technically, I had. I was later told that the teacher had asked the other pupils in my class where I was but no one had any idea that I was just standing behind this wardrobe for the whole school day.

It all boiled down to the fact that I was really nervous of school at the beginning. I didn't know many of the pupils and it was all a bit of a daunting experience for me. I think it didn't actually help living so close to the school. I had grown up seeing what it was like over the garden fence and rather than be intrigued, I came to look at it with a sense of trepidation.

Thankfully, better the devil you know and all that, I eventually settled into school life—of course, I had little choice. I started doing quite well, even excelling in subjects such as maths and English.

One day, we were visited by some important-looking people from England who gave us a talk about the country. Being so young, I didn't really understand why they kept eulogising about the Royal Family and London, the sights and sounds. For me, it just looked like a faraway, prosperous land where, literally, kings and queens lived.

But their motive was to try and sell England to us. They were looking for families to go and move there to work in hospitals and the railways. Part of this propaganda was to convince the youngsters on the island that England was the place to be so they would both move and, just as importantly, stay there. As coincidence happens, my parents were already considering moving to England believing it would give us a better life.

As innocent school children, we already considered England as our Mother country. Not that we had a lot of choice in this way of thinking. In school, we were always taught to behave like we were British with the teachers even claiming Trinidad had no history. All our books had come from England and it was something we accepted without any question or trouble—there was no reason for impressionable school kids to query it.

These dignitaries told us all about England, they told us the streets were paved with gold. At the same time, they were luring adults with the incentive of regular work and more money.

We were shown a film showcasing the country, full of strong Union Jack images and I remember seeing the posh parts of Chelsea. Being about five or six years old, I was completely fazed by the sights and sounds, everything looked so beautiful. It was clearly all propaganda but we had no reason not to believe them, so it worked a treat.

That said we didn't move straight away. We went to San Fernando first where my Mum established the successful hair salon. To a young boy, this was like a different world with all the strange devices and, sometimes, even stranger women. I can recall a stove in the salon which would be used to heat the combs with lots of grease on the girls' hair to straighten it out. Some of the local families may have struggled for money but these women sure wanted to look good.

My Dad had more of an unusual job. He was a rabies inspector in San Fernando which meant he had to catch bats to stop them attacking the cows. He would test the bats for rabies and then bring home any dead ones in little bottles. There we would be eating our dinner with these dead animals in jars staring at us from the mantelpiece.

My parents were doing ok. We had a Morris Traveller and my Dad had a Triumph motorbike. I can remember being so happy when he got home from work one day that I raced out to see him and grabbed the motorcycle exhaust. It was literally red hot and my hand stuck to it causing some flesh to come off. I screamed and was in floods of tears. I never had a scooter or a motorbike when I was older—I think being literally scarred for life was the reason. I guess moving to England was still in my parents' minds but they wanted to be successful and have a financial cushion behind them before they made the daunting decision.

For me, I was never scared about the prospect of moving more than 4,000 miles away. Even in Trinidad, I was always surrounded by English people. The nearby town of Pointe-a-Pierre now boasts the country's largest oil refinery and was actually built for and populated by employees of the company. When I was growing up, the area was a hive of English people who had come over to work.

The whole racial culture in Trinidad was a lot more integrated than it was in England at the time. You didn't batter an eyelid at seeing white boys in Trinidad and I think this is what made me think from an early age that everyone was equal. It was certainly a reason why I was taken aback a little by some of the confrontations I had when we did eventually move to London.

I made a lot of friends with the boys who went to the same school as me. We mixed well, especially when England came to Trinidad and played the West Indies at cricket. These were always exciting occasions and we would all have a fantastic time together, white or black, no matter who you were supporting.

The school would give us all a day off so we could watch the cricket and my favourite player was Len Hutton, England captain at that time. It would always make my day when I saw him confidently stride out onto the pitch.

He was such a graceful cricketer and I can recall him batting for such a long time that the West Indians grew more and more frustrated by their failed efforts to get him out.

This impatience started to manifest itself in the crowd, many of whom had spent the day drinking rum, as they were prone to do.

They thought their big moment had come when there was a huge shout for LBW. Finally it seemed Hutton's resistance had been broken and the West Indians had claimed their scalp. Not so said the umpires who waved away the appeals—sparking pandemonium in the crowd. All hell broke loose, bottles were flying everywhere and I got hit on the back by one. It hurt for weeks.

It was in San Fernando that I had my first chance meeting with a celebrity, well someone who was destined to become one. The name Hasely Crawford might not be well-known to everyone but he is a national hero in Trinidad. Not that I had any inkling of what the future held in store for young Hasely as we ran and fought, like kids do.

We were quite good friends and our families became close before we moved to England. About 20 years later, we were living in Thetford when on my little portable television I saw Hasely win the 100 metres to become the first Olympic champion ever from our homeland. It was pretty mind-blowing to say the least. My mind wandered back to when we used to fight and he would hit me and run off. Who knew that I was one of the first to help him hone his speed?

Now here I was cheering him on from my armchair. When he won the gold medal, the first thing I did was phone my brother who by then had moved back to Trinidad. He said the country was going crazy and that there was going to be street parties and everything. Hasely's achievements really united the whole country. Quite rightly, he was nothing short of a national hero in Trinidad and they even named a stadium after him in Port of Spain.

As I messed around with a future Olympic champion, my Mum still retained realistic dreams of moving to England and making an even better life for her family. But my Dad was a lot more laid back about everything.

Clive Bernard was born in 1916. He was very quiet, not one to make a fuss. That's not to say that he was a pushover. If we ever did anything naughty, he could be very strict with us—it would be bang and we'd have the belt. But he was a fair man and I only have memories of good times with my Dad.

My childhood had its ups and downs but overall it was a happy one. Sometimes I think I was a little too sheltered and I didn't know enough about life outside my family home. When I started making a name for myself in the West End, I quickly realised that not everything is so idyllic and that things don't always turn out the way you want. I had to learn this the hard way. I can't complain though as compared to other families you see and read about, I had a good time growing up. Sometimes I wish I was back living in those carefree days in Trinidad.

Unlike my mother, my Dad's background was hazier. He didn't talk much about it which invariably meant we felt we couldn't bring it up. We knew he had grown up with his aunt in Santa Cruz, a small town in Trinidad and Tobago where cricket legend Brian Lara was born. I only met my Dad's mother once—and I had to wait until she was 94 to do it.

I had always suspected there had been some kind of family rift that my parents didn't want me to know about. They certainly never talked about it and I am still none the wiser today.

My wife Doreen and I had gone back to the homeland for a holiday when out of the blue, my Dad said he was taking me to see my Nan. I think it meant a lot to him for me to see her before she passed away.

Having not seen my grandmother for as long as I could remember, I felt a little apprehensive as we drove up to her house. But we were met with a far greater obstacle than nerves and not knowing what to say as she wouldn't come out of her home.

Had an emotional family moment become too much for her, I wondered. In fact, the real reason was far less serious and much more to do with simple female vanity. "She's putting her wig on", my aunt reliably informed us, ending any sense of trepidation in an instant. Once such dramas were solved, it was a lovely occasion and my Nan eventually lived on well beyond 100.

I think my parents were a classic case of opposites attract. When they decided to get married, my Dad believed in doing it properly. But there were no phones in those days and they lived quite some distance apart so it posed a problem when my Dad wanted to ask his future father-in-law for his daughter's hand in marriage. Undeterred, my Dad decided to write him a letter.

The letter was dated 21st March 1941 and read:

Dear Mr Pinder,

You have no doubt observed that I am a frequent visitor to your home and that as a result a close friendship has sprung up between your daughter Mildred and myself.

As a matter of fact as a result of that friendship, I have been able from time to time to discern in those qualities which in my humble opinion go to make a perfect companion.

After a great deal of serious thought therefore, I have thought it wise to solicit of you her hand in matrimony with the hope that my proposal will meet with your approval.

Should you accept my proposal, I can assure you that I will be quite ready and willing to have the nuptial rites solemnised within two years from the date of your acceptance of my proposal, and I take this opportunity to assure you that you will at no time whatsoever have the cause to regret that you permitted your daughter to be under my protection.

Thanking you in anticipation for an early and favourable reply.

I remain,

Yours faithfully,

Clive Bernard.

It is hard enough asking your future father-in-law for his daughter's hand in marriage at the best of times. I can only imagine what It was like waiting for a response to a letter. Looking back on this, it is almost like a different world. Most young people today wouldn't even know what that words "nuptial rites solemnised" means. But it also makes me very proud of my father. He obviously had a lot of respect for tradition and he clearly took the letter, and therefore the marriage proposal, very serious. His use of words and phrases showed he took time in writing the letter and it is nice to think he wanted to marry my mother that much to go to so much trouble.

Although his constant reference to the word proposal when he writes to my granddad seems to suggest my mother would have little choice in the decision to "solemnise any nuptial rites". As for giving a date of when the wedding would take place, as if it was some kind of completion date, it is almost like a bank letter or some form of work taking place.

It did make me smile when I was shown this letter for the first time. Fortunately, my father's grasp of the English language worked and the reply from his future-in-law was favourable.

They were not the most openly romantic couple but you could tell they loved each other. And they loved their children very much.

My brother Ansel certainly got the family's height genes compared to me while my sister looked like Diana Ross when she was younger. Growing up, we were just normal kids. We would fight and argue at times but we would be quite close, even if we didn't always show it. After moving to London, my brother passed his 11-plus exams but they wouldn't put him into grammar school. It was in the 1950s and although the school never gave a reason, we always felt it was because of his colour.

My Mum was furious and demanded answers from anyone and everyone. Typical feisty Mum, only wanting the best for her family. But in the end, the school board refused to change their mind. Fortunately, it made little difference. Ansel was very bright, becoming a prefect at school before getting a job working for the government. One of his roles was to answer letters in support of Enoch Powell after the politician made his controversial 'rivers of blood' speech. I am not sure I could have done it with the same grace and dignity that Ansel has shown throughout his whole life.

The one thing the three of us rarely talked about was any racial issues we might have encountered. My first memories of problems were largely centred on my time at secondary school, but I never told anyone, I just kept it in. It was only when we were adults that I first mentioned to Barbara about the taunts and name-calling that I had endured. My sister was also clever and travelled all over the world. She was like my Mum in that sense, fearless, and she worked in various embassies which meant she saw quite a few places.

Although Ansel returned to Trinidad, his mark in this area had been made after he worked in the office of Lord Aberdare, the former speaker of the House of Lords, and accompanied him to the opening of the West Suffolk Hospital in Bury St Edmunds. It was quite fitting that it was at that particular hospital that Doreen received so much care and support before she was later transferred to St Nicholas Hospice Care.

Like my brother, Barbara also returned to Trinidad but the three of us remain close. I know if I needed to talk to someone, they are always on the end of the phone despite all the hundreds of miles between us—you can't ask for more than that really.

Chapter 2: My Treacherous Trip To England

The day finally arrived when my Mum decided she wanted to broaden our horizons and move to England. Although she had not been completely persuaded by the film propaganda, the seeds had certainly been sown. After she had made a success of her life in Trinidad, she wanted to do exactly the same for herself and her family in a much bigger, and more daunting, country.

Of course I was too young to appreciate it at the time, but my Mum was championing women's rights, even if it wasn't deliberate on her part. At that time, she was doing something that no woman would contemplate doing and I am very proud of her for that.

When she passed away from a stroke in April 2003, the local newspaper in Trinidad wrote a glowing tribute about her spirit and the fact she wasn't willing just to settle for anything but the very best when it came to providing for her children.

My Dad felt the same but he was a little more laidback in his demeanour. Not my Mum though. She wanted to make sure her three children had every possible chance in life and for her that meant only one thing, going to England.

I'm proud of her for doing it, but looking back I'm not altogether surprised. She was a very strong-willed woman who was a success at whatever she set her mind to. Typical of their personalities, my Mum was more of a driving force behind the move while my Dad's demeanour about pretty much anything life threw at him was a trait that I copy to this very day. That said, getting on a ship to England on her own was probably the bravest thing my Mum ever did in her life and a decision that would eventually lead me to an unimaginable world to the one I would leave behind in the Caribbean.

Our journey getting there was not without its problems. Because there was something of the unknown about England, and because they had three young children, my parents decided only one of them should move, test the water and then report back before traipsing their young across the other side of the world.

It was my Mum who bravely made the journey on her own at the relatively tender age of 31 years old. This might seem strange to some who think that my Dad should have acted like the head of the household. But to me, it just typified his laid-back manner and her strong will. I can imagine him being non-plussed about the thought of sailing to a foreign country while my Mum would have been desperately keen to experience new things and hopefully be a success.

Given that imbalance in their personalities and desire, it would have been decided that my Mum should make the move first. In fact, my Dad might not even have had a choice. This meant my Dad had to look after me and my brother and sister while my Mum ventured to England all by herself. Of course, a woman making the trip on her own was uncommon in 1952 and she probably got some strange looks en-route.

It was often the case that the man would come over to England first and get a job before bringing his family over to settle. But my Mum wouldn't have cared a jot about such reactions, she would have just been dreaming about what lay ahead. This unusual decision by my Mum just proved what she was like—determined, occasionally feisty, and always wanting to make the life of her family as good as possible. That was my Mum.

But there was also something inherent in my Mum when it came to travelling. Even when we settled in England, she would still go off to places like America and Canada for holidays. She was actually in America when Elvis Presley first broke onto the scene and she can remember some black people criticising him for doing what they described as 'our music'.

But with all these adventures, she once again would be travelling solo as my Dad was never one for experiencing foreign holidays. I sometimes think he missed out on seeing things but I prefer to focus on her bravery to want to see other parts of the world.

In those days, the only way to come to England was on a boat and I can remember seeing her leave on this rickety thing that looked like an old trawler packed with West Indians. In the end, she lived in England on her own for three long years. I was only six at the time and though I missed my Mum a lot, I always knew that we would be reunited as a family again. The four of us were living with my grandparents at the time in Diego Martin and we were always being reassured that we would see our Mum again.

While he tried to hide it, my Dad missed her terribly. He would cry a lot but always try and put on a brave face when we were around. Sometimes we would catch him upset and he would tell us how much he was missing Mum. It was a tough time for us all.

The only way my parents could contact each other was through letter and Mum wrote a lot telling us all about England and how much she was missing us all. This wasn't the same as actually having her with us, but it was a small sense of comfort that we were able to keep with us until the next letter arrived.

Upon arriving in England, she had settled in Harlesden with an old school friend Dr David Pitt, who would later become Lord Pitt and be the longest serving black parliamentarian. He was instrumental in ensuring my Mum settled into London life for the three years she lived there on her own.

It was in 1955 when it was decided that the time was right to join up with my Mum in England and be reunited again as a family.

I can remember being excited and a little anxious by going to this big new country. But most of all, I was just happy to be seeing my Mum again and for my parents to be together once more.

But not everyone was happy that we were leaving. Before we left, my Granddad said that he would never see us again and he even locked himself in his room so he didn't have to say goodbye. I was too small to understand why he was so upset, but he was right—we did never see him again.

My Grandmother, on the other hand, came to see us off and we set sail aboard the Fyffe's liner The Convener. As some of the only children on the boat, you would imagine it would be a big adventure for wide-eyed youngsters who had never experienced such a thing. The reality couldn't have been more different. The initial smooth and lovely Caribbean waters soon turned into a nightmare when we hit the Atlantic.

We were sailing in November so it was always going to be a bit choppy. But what transpired was a lot, lot worse. The boat seemed like a little rocking matchbox as the waves crashed over it. There was all this lovely food laid out on the tables, everything you could think of, but all we could stomach was crackers and steam fish. It was a complete waste of the lavish spread that had been offered to everyone on the boat. We spent most of the time it took to get to Southampton confined to our cabins because as soon as we went on deck, we were sick again. My Dad must have gone through hell, feeling equally ill but worrying about us at the same time, during what proved to be a gruelling three-week journey.

The London streets might have been "paved with gold", but getting there was an arduous experience.

How we ended up in England in one piece still amazes me. When we arrived in Southampton, it was cold and foggy and of course this was the first time any of us had seen fog. It was a gloomy scene in keeping with the journey that had got us to this foreign land.

But everything we had gone through quickly vanished as soon as I saw my Mum and was in her arms once again. We were taken to Dr Pitt's house where we stayed for a while. He was a very distinguished gentleman, a really big chap with thick long hair and silver on the side.

As soon as we got settled in England my Dad went straight out and bought a television. I had already experienced the wonder of moving images thanks to films back in Trinidad. My favourite actor was Norman Wisdom whose films were always shown in my homeland. He was very popular with all the school kids and everyone loved his role as Norman Pitkin against frustrated boss Mr Grimsdale. I found him really funny and I loved the slapstick of him throwing himself around. When we lived in Diego Martin, we were within walking distance of the cinema and every time his films were shown, I always made sure I saw them.

I would no longer have to walk anywhere after my Dad decided to buy a television and it was to prove key in my musical development. One of my first memories was seeing a guy on the screen singing The Garden of Eden. It was Frankie Vaughan and he was on a show called Cool for Cats which was presented by Ken

Walton, who later became famous for wrestling on ITV. Frankie had this white suit and was kicking his leg out in time with the music. I had never seen entertainment like it, I hadn't even seen a white suit before. He was a real entertainer and had played in places like the London Palladium. He really impressed me. It was then I realised what I wanted to do and who I wanted to be like. I wanted to be the next Frankie Vaughan.

My parents were soon well aware of my burgeoning love of music, it was impossible not to be. I remember seeing the great Frank Sinatra on the cover of a magazine and asking my Dad whether he thought I could ever sing like Ol' Blue Eyes. Opting for a realistic and blunt approach, my Dad simply told me not to be so stupid. So much for a softly-softly answer for a stardom-seeking youth.

Not realising that Sinatra was one in a million, I was actually a little cross with his response. I liked singing, I thought I had a good voice and even if I was a young boy on a Caribbean island, who's to say I couldn't be the next Frank Sinatra? However, while he had doubts whether I would become as successful as a Grammy Lifetime Achievement Award, Oscar-winning member of the Rat Pack, my Dad was still keen on fuelling my interest in music.

He bought me a toy guitar but I quickly learned that instruments and me were not meant to go together. I was only really interested in singing, but that was difficult in a country where actual song lyrics, let alone musical accompaniment, were difficult to come by.

When I could, I would buy songsheets which would have the words of famous songs of the time, but no music. This would keep my interest up but I longed for more. Though I didn't know it when I first moved there, England would provide me with a lifetime of opportunities and experiences that I never even knew existed when I was a small boy in Trinidad.

We stayed with Dr Pitt for well over a year. Harlesden was a good place to live and we didn't experience much racial trouble. The worst the kids would say was that my teeth were so white because my skin was black, but I didn't let anything like that bother me. I was certainly going to hear a lot worse as I got older.

From Harlesden, we moved to Fulham and I became one of the only black people at Parsons Green Primary School. I once again got on fine with the other children and also in school. I played football and cricket and even had a trial with Crystal Palace Football Club. I became really keen on athletics with the 100 metres my speciality. Perhaps those times playing with Hasely had rubbed off on me, even if the thought of me now running 10 metres brings me out in a cold sweat.

After a while, my Mum and Dad, who had settled well in London, decided it was time to move out of Dr Pitt's and buy a house. They had a look round a house in Bell Green, Sydenham, and thought it was the perfect place to buy their first home in England. It never occurred to them that there would be a major snag with their house-hunting. It came when the person selling the house clapped eyes on my parents for the first time.

Within an instant, he had called off the sale despite the fact that my Mum and Dad had the finances to go through with it. It seemed like a black person's money wasn't good enough to buy this particular home.

Fortunately, my Dad was a nice bloke and well-liked. While my Mum worked at the railways at Liverpool Street, he had a good job for a private shopping company close by. His boss, an old Army colonel, Mr Parsons, really liked him. My parents only ever referred to Mr and Mrs Parsons so to this day I am oblivious about their first names.

It was in keeping with how I felt about them to be honest. Mr Parsons scared me a little. I think it was his army roots and his army moustache. But he really respected my Dad. There was one time when his company was going to merge with another but had doubts when they saw my Dad who was by then a director. It seemed they had problems dealing with a black man so Mr Parsons immediately called off any hopes of a business deal.

After hearing about his problems buying a house, Mr Parsons told my Dad that the next time they saw a house they really liked, they should keep out of the limelight. He said he would handle all the arrangements and my parents would then pay him back. My boss bought the house in Bell Green and the previous owners never knew it was my Dad who moved in.

We could always count on Mr Parsons for support. But it worked both ways. My Dad and his boss were kindred spirits who would always look out for each other. My Dad was quiet and calm and he always got on with people when we moved to England. Through diligent saving, and of course hard work, my parents actually became Trinidadian dollar millionaires, but there was never any airs or graces about them. They were never flash, never allowed money to change them and they would always preach the value of hard work to their children. Even when they were offered something for free, like the time Mr Parsons offered us the use of his holiday home in Felixstowe for free, my Dad would always say 'thanks but no thanks' preferring to work hard for everything we got.

We were the first black people to move into the area and the one thing that struck me about the houses was that there was no bathroom. While we didn't live a palatial lifestyle in Trinidad, everyone had showers and the fact that we moved somewhere without one was strange to me. For people who didn't have a bath, the best option was to have one in the public baths scattered around everywhere. The problem for me was that I used to be taunted by the operators of these places. They would give me soap and a towel, but when I came out they would say that I didn't look any cleaner, things like that. Once again, I ignored the insults. They were looking for a reaction and I wasn't about to give them the satisfaction. My Mum and Dad worked very hard and eventually built an extension onto the back of the house and put a bathroom in. When they did this, some of our neighbours were clearly jealous and quickly copied them.

In those days, small-minded white folk gave the impression that they viewed our family as dirty and that our house must be some kind of squalid mess. No one would ever say it to our face, but you knew this is what people were thinking. One time we had a routine visit by some social officers and they couldn't believe how clean our house was. But to us, of course, it was just normal home run by clean-living people.

People used to say to me that we didn't fit in around here. But what they didn't know was that my grandfather fought in World War One for this country. He volunteered for service and fought in the trenches. He would sometimes tell me stories about his time during the conflict and when his sons came to England to study, they brought his medals with them to show us. Leon Pinder was a true hero.

Chapter Three: First Impressions

I might not have been the smartest student or the best behaved at school, but I will never forget my time at primary school as it was then that I first met Doreen Hatcher.

I was never one for believing in fate. But when my Mum and Dad bought the house in Sydenham, there was a girl living across the road who grabbed my eye. Well to be honest, it was her pony tail that did it, that was all. I used to see her going to the school and I would always notice her pony tail. It is such a small thing and a strange reason to like someone. Maybe it was because I hadn't seen something like that before, even at my Mum's hair salon in Trinidad. I was only 12 years old and it did the trick for me.

Doreen lived close by with her parents but I didn't see her that much as we went to different schools. I was at Sedge Hill Secondary School at the time and Doreen went to a nice school in Forest Hill. But every time our paths would cross, it would always brighten my day. To the point, that I started making sure our paths crossed more and more regularly.

There was something about her that caught my eye and I really wanted to ask her out. I knew that Doreen had a sister, Carol, who I thought would be a perfect way-in to me asking Doreen out. In truth, I wasn't brave enough just to walk up and ask Doreen myself. I think being two close sisters, they just wanted to have a little fun with me. When I asked Carol what her sister's name was, she claimed it was Michelle. I later found out that Doreen wasn't too keen on her first name when she was younger but at the time, I thought they were enjoying giving me the run-around a little.

Fortunately, Doreen must have been a little bit interested and we began to hang out together as friends. I was learning to play the guitar at the time and I invited Doreen and her friend, Lana, over to listen to me. The first song I learnt on the guitar was Danny Boy but Doreen wasn't having any of it. She wasn't that impressed, in fact she didn't fancy me at all at first. Her friend Lana fancied me instead.

Eventually, we did start going out though. It must have been all the pestering that did it. She changed her mind and we started spending a lot of time together. We would often go cycling and ride miles all over south London to places like Sevenoaks and Tunbridge Wells. We used to go to a park in Bell Green where people would play cricket. I can remember there was a chocolate factory sited next to the park and they would make all these different kinds of confectionary. We used to climb on boxes and sneak over the fence to take some of the chocolate. It was harmless really and it sure tasted good.

I bought a bike for £14, which was a lot of money at the time. We would cycle everywhere and we never encountered any trouble over a black boy cycling with a white girl. Well not that we knew of anyway. It certainly never occurred to either of us that it could be a strange sight.

We started going together properly when we were 13 and it just grew from there. We never spoke about colour and our parents certainly never mentioned it. Of course, it was quite rare to see a black person going out with a white person but her family were perfect and never mentioned it. My parents absolutely loved Doreen and would always tell me what a great girl she was and how I should never let her go.

Our colour never came up as an issue, it certainly never bothered us. If someone didn't like it or didn't like us being together, we never got angry, we just never thought about it.

Doreen eventually moved in with me and my parents. She had a big family and their house was pretty camped. When my sister moved to Canada to work, it gave us the perfect chance to move in together, albeit with my Mum and Dad as well.

She lived in the spare room upstairs and I lived in a separate room downstairs. There was the odd occasion we would sneak into each other's room and while we tried to be coy and clever, my Dad did catch me once. He didn't say too much and I think he never even told Mum about the liaison going on under their roof.

As we got older, we never looked at anyone else and we were really happy. Her parents would come over for Christmas and we got on really well.

Her Dad, Henry Arthur Hatcher, was in the Second World War, when he was really young, about 15 or so. He told me that he was fighting in the trenches when he dropped his rifle. When he went back for it, he got shot in the knee. He was lucky not to be killed and his mother actually got a letter saying that he had died in battle. A few years later, he turned up at her door and she fainted. I'm not surprised really. It must have been an awful shock, especially after she had grieved for him. He used to show me where he got shot. It never properly healed. He lived until his 70s and every single day up to his death, he would have to dress the wound. He had a very special relationship with Doreen who also had three sisters, one brother and one half-sister. She looked upon him as the bee's knees and it was mutual.

Despite the injury, he remained a very hard working, seemingly working every single day, even Christmas and New Year. He drove a lorry for the gas works in Bell Green, although in those days you didn't have to take and pass a driving test. You went for the job, got in a lorry and within five minutes you were driving. It seems crazy to think about that now, but then it just seemed the accepted thing.

Aside from meeting the love of my life, school was not always an easy time for me.

My problems started when I went to Sedge Hill. I had trouble with one or two of the teachers who seemingly refused to teach me. They would have no problem telling my classmates, who were all white, that they had a problem with me. I don't know if they thought I was going to be trouble or what their issue was. I just kept these difficulties to myself. Maybe I should have told my parents, but I didn't want to worry them or get them involved.

I remember once winning a competition in our woodwork class to make a guitar. With music now well and truly in my heart and soul, it was obviously a project I was very interested in and took a lot of time and care over. My guitar was well crafted and I deserved to win—one teacher even told me so. But sadly the music teacher wouldn't acknowledge that mine was good, he even let out a huge sigh in front of the rest of the class when he could see that my guitar was the best. But this type of thing was common at Sedge Hill in those days, as I am sure it was in many schools in London.

It was just full of really stupid incidents. The headmaster was told that I was a chain-smoker when I had never touched a cigarette in my life. One teacher used to say that he could tell by looking at my fingers—it was almost comical, if a little bit hurtful at the same time. They had dance lessons at the school and I was always the last one to get chosen by the girls. My dance partner was always the least attractive and eventually she got fed up of dancing with me and refused. This didn't exactly make me want to attend dance lessons all the time, so there would be occasions when I would just stay in the classroom rather than turn up for the lessons. This move would only get me in trouble with the headmaster who had been told by the teacher that I had skipped practice. I told the headmaster that the girls didn't want to dance with me, but I still got the cane. Eventually, some of the girls realised that I was not actually a bad person and started dancing with me. But as soon as that happened, the dance lessons stopped without any explanation.

My brother and sister also had problems and their own stories to tell, but it seemed like I was picked out, and picked on, a little more than them. To this day, I have no idea why that was. Perhaps certain teachers were looking to get a reaction out of me, but I was just like my father. Placid, laid-back, perhaps too much for my own good sometimes. All I was interested in was music, not petty comments from teachers or a fellow pupil. I never spoke to anyone about these problems, not to my parents nor my brother and sister. I just kept it inside—the same as I did when I entered the music business.

I can't blame the teachers for everything though. There were times that I would skip school completely and, unsurprisingly, it was music's fault.

When I was 15, I had to decide whether to leave Sedge Hill or carry on and do my GCE exams. Though they were well aware of how much music meant to me, my parents wanted me to stay on at school. Perhaps if they had known some of the problems I had to endure, they might have been less keen. I, on the other hand, was certain I wanted to leave school and the sooner the better.

In hindsight, I should have done my exams but I didn't think I was bright enough to do well in a classroom. I wanted to get into electronics and work on amplifiers but I got a little bit confused and actually started an apprenticeship as an electrician.

It was not a very enjoyable experience. I worked under some good people but often, when I was on building sites, I would be taught very little. Unless you describe sweeping and making tea all day long an apprenticeship. I think I was viewed as an outsider, largely because of my colour, and I was never given a chance to learn any skills and prove myself.

It was not long before I was not putting in the required effort. Deep down, it was not what I wanted to do but if I had the right training and good people helping me, I would have given it my best shot.

My worst moment was when I was told to move a reel of big cable which was wrapped around an iron wheel all by myself. Predictably, I couldn't, so they called me a "disgrace to your race". I was used to the racist comments by then. It was pretty shocking stuff really.

I think it was a relief to all parties when they decided to let me go. They said I was stopping another lad from getting an apprenticeship that he could really benefit from. For once, we were in total agreement. They knew I wanted to be a singer even though I needed a back-up in case the music didn't take off. But becoming an electrician was not the answer.

Doreen was always very supportive of my musical aspirations. There were good times, of course, even when the money wasn't exactly rolling in. But there was also some very difficult times when the music wasn't quite taking off.

Throughout it all, I could always count on Doreen's support and backing. There was also the potential problem of other girls' interest, the groupies who used to hang around the band. I wasn't a bad-looking lad when I was younger and mixing in musical circles meant you were always likely to get some attraction. Some girls used to hang around but it didn't mean anything and Doreen knew that.

We ended up getting engaged. I wasn't the most romantic person in the world but I just knew that I wanted to marry Doreen. There was no grand proposal and I didn't have to write a letter to her father like my own Dad did.

Doreen's father was very shy and I think would have been embarrassed had I spoken to him first. But the one thing we could always count on was the constant support of both our families. Neither of us saw our colour as an issue and fortunately our families thought exactly the same.

We were living together at my parents' house and one day my Mum and Dad said: "Isn't it about time you two got married?" And that's how it came about. As I said, I wouldn't have won any prizes for romance, but it just seemed like the natural step for us, which I guess is romantic in itself. We must have done something right as we were married for a total of 41 years.

Chapter Four: Hooked On music

Whether it was annoying my parents or trying to serenade Doreen, my love of music kept growing.

It had started in Trinidad where youngsters were often reliant on the radio in the days of no television.

I was about five years old when I used to listen to a little-known station called Radio Fusion and heard the likes of Frank Sinatra and Nat King Cole. I had never heard anything like it in my life. They were so soulful with their voices and so meaningful with their words.

Songs I particularly liked included Young at Heart by Frank Sinatra and Nat King Cole's Pretend and They Tried To Tell Us We're Too Young. Sometimes at the weekend, my Mum and Dad would take us to Port of Spain and I'd buy little music sheets. They would have no music score on the paper, only the lyrics, but I used them to learn the songs I had heard on the radio. From then on, you couldn't stop me singing. It was often to myself or at my family who showed remarkable patience when I am sure they wanted a moment's peace.

I wanted to be just as famous as these people, perhaps not having the full appreciation of how great the likes of Nat King Cole were. It was of course virtually an impossible wish. There is only one Frank Sinatra after all, but I share the same love of music that these people had and I am happy to have that in common with these great performers.

My passion for music hadn't gone unnoticed. When I started at Parsons Green Primary School in London, other kids soon realised that I liked singing and some would even ask me for a quick rendition. It was from these early seeds that my love of performing started to grow.

It was not that I thought I was particularly good. I just enjoyed singing, simple as that. So when my fellow pupils asked for a little song, I was only too happy to oblige.

I would always sing The Garden of Eden. Seeing Frankie Vaughan on television really made an impression on me and from that day on I have always loved his music. I think the song also suited my voice and it is one of my regrets that I have never recorded it myself.

Singing at such a young age, I had no idea about the meaning of the lyrics or how a song was constructed—I just liked the music and the melody.

From these little experiences, my performing skills improved and it gave me a real confidence boost.

I would sing at every chance I got. It was not something I necessarily inherited from my parents. My Mum was never that interested in singing while my Dad was only ever interested in listening to music. Bing Crosby was one of his favourites.

My grandma used to sing in the Anglican Church choir and my brother and sister sung in a gospel choir but that didn't interest me at all. I wanted to perform and would even put on a show when I was washing up, even if it meant just singing loudly to myself.

Beyond singing to some school friends, there were few opportunities for me at school although it was no surprise that I got on well with my music teacher at Parsons Green.

As well as complimenting my voice, he once commented in my school report that I had a great personality. This is something I have always tried to get across whenever I am performing, whether in a swinging London club in the 1960s or playing a smaller venue in Norfolk, close to where I now live. I also got on well with the English teacher as I enjoyed the subject, but it was not always the same story with some teachers appearing to take a dislike to me.

I would often day-dream in the classroom, usually about music, and near the end of my schooling, I would skip classes altogether, taking the train to the West End and visiting record shops.

I found what became music gold in the shape of a record shop in Charing Cross Road which effectively shaped what I would listen to as I went through my teenage years.

As a lot of the artists and albums remained strangers to me, I would have no choice but to be persuaded by record covers. It might seem a strange way to buy music but through it I uncovered the likes of James Brown and the Isley Brothers.

It was in another music shop, Len's Stiles in Lewisham, where I met my first ever jamming partner. Pete London and I clicked straight away. I didn't know it then but Len's Stiles went on to be part of Lewisham Town Centre for 65 years and would become famous for attracting the likes of Status Quo, Manfred Mann and Bill Wyman's Rhythm Kings as customers to the shop. It also paid an integral part in my development as it led to the eventual formation of my first band.

Pete and I started to jam together although we had no thoughts of starting a band at first. He was a big fan of Gene Vincent and the Blue Caps and we used to go to his house and perform Be-Bop-a-Lula. It was around 1958 and I can remember watching a show called Oh Boy which was on ITV and broadcast live from the Hackney Empire. It was largely credited for discovering Cliff Richard. We used to love the show as it was aimed at a young rock 'n' roll audience. Cliff would copy Elvis Presley down to a tee. He would be on the show every week and he became really popular through it. Cliff impressed me as a performer and he was smart and had a great business head. He was the only one who recorded original material rather than American songs. But I wasn't keen on his type of music.

Because he was so successful and popular, every band wanted to be like Cliff and The Shadows. Well everyone except me. I had my eyes on the real deal and that meant Elvis. When the man who would become King came along, it completely knocked me out. I, and every youngster my age, had been used to the likes of Frank Sinatra, Nat King Cole and Dean Martin, all true greats. But Heartbreak Hotel was something else. I didn't even know that kind of music was possible. After hearing it, I would always keep an eye out for anything new by Elvis. The first time I heard That's All Right on the radio, I went out and bought it straight away.

While still a raw and quite nervous performer, I decided that I wanted to start taking music a little more seriously and that meant performing to a larger crowd than just Pete. One show I was particularly keen on was Hughie Green's Opportunity Knocks. It became a big hit on the television, but more often that not I listened to it on Radio Luxembourg. Perhaps listening to it isn't quite the right description. Sometimes all I would hear was just static as the station had a few problems with reception at the time.

It was when I heard Doris Day's Secret Love that I took the bold step of applying to go on the show. I was accepted but soon realised that this particularl opportunity had come way too early for me. I had decided to sing the same song she had won an Oscar with following her role in Calamity Jane. The only problem was that I had no idea what key Secret Love was in. In fact I knew nothing about music keys at all. All I was armed with was the music sheet. The audition was held in a studio in London. It was the biggest thing I had done to date, but it was unsurprisingly a disaster.

I sang in one key and the pianist played in another and the whole thing was just awful.

Despite this setback, I was officially hooked on music and performing. With me not really excelling at school, I knew pretty early on that I wanted to sing for a living. The only snag was that I didn't have a clue how I could achieve this. The Opportunity Knocks gig had given me a taster, but it had also shown up how naïve I was regarding the whole industry and how much improvement I needed to make.

I wrote to lots of agents hoping to get a big break, but not really knowing what I was doing. There was one agent, a big Jewish chap, Dick Catts, who would always advertise in The Stage for talent to contact him. I was an avid reader of the magazine so I wrote to this man and he agreed to see me. Once again, this audition had its fair share of problems. Being a big Elvis fan, I decided to sing Teddy Bear and Don't Be Cruel over the top of the voice of the King. On the day in question, I carried my Grundig recorder up to his office and started singing.

But within a few moments, he stopped me and asked who the person singing in the background was. Not wanting to reveal the identity of a certain E. Presley and make myself look stupid, I acted dumb and mumbled something about how it was a recording of me singing the song and that I was doubling my voice. It was cheeky of me to claim that it was my voice rather than the future King of Rock 'n' Roll but I panicked. It was pure nerves. I was desperate to impress but I had got well and truly busted.

Dick knew it was Elvis but decided to test me. Suffice to say I failed, or so I thought. I somehow had managed to impress him a little as he phoned the manager of one of the top artists of the time and said he had a young man in his office who might have potential. Despite my little white lie, he had spotted something in my voice and my performance. But any hopes of a big break, or even a glimmer of one, were quickly dashed when the interest on the other end of the phone cooled when he heard that I was black.

It was the first time, but certainly not the last, that my colour would be a problem in someone's eyes in the music industry. It hurt initially but it also made me stronger. I was never a confident person but I had done enough to impress one agent that I had something. Of course, I was raw. But it wasn't a complete failure.

Bonded by our love of music, Pete and I became good friends. And we would soon become a threesome. One day we were walking past the Tigers Head pub in Lee Green when I heard a guitarist playing in the cellar.

Pete knew who it was and introduced me to Albert Lee, a man who would later become an internationally renowned musician, described by Eric Clapton no less as "the greatest guitarist in the world". I started singing with Albert in the pub cellar every Friday night with me thinking I was Elvis and Albert thinking he was Scotty

Moore, Elvis's guitarist. They were good times and we were learning as we went, eventually thinking we sounded pretty good.

With Pete and Albert on guitar and me performing the vocals, we decided to form a band, The Thunderbeats. This was again not without its pitfalls, the first being that we couldn't find anyone to buy an amplifier for us from the local record shop. We wanted to buy it on HP as it was £40 which was a lot of money in those days, but showed how serious we were taking our fledgling band. We were too young to do it ourselves but fortunately my kind Dad stepped in and agreed to be the signature to allow us to buy a Vox amplifier.

I had never sung with anyone before and I was out of tune and out of my depth to be perfectly honest. It was 1959 and we played in bars and ballrooms around South London, doing songs like Move It, Travelling Light and the Young Ones but it didn't suit my voice at all. I just couldn't sing them and sounded flat all the time.

It was funny because some of the venues we played in were ones that I had previously not been allowed in before because they only let white people in. But when I became the lead singer of the band playing on a particular night, they had little choice but to let me through.

Though I had wanted to be in a band since I first started taking music seriously, I never enjoyed my time in The Thunderbeats. To be honest it was quite a relief when I got the sack. I had only been in a band for about a year and I had been given the boot. Fortunately, I wasn't the type of person to get too demoralised and I certainly couldn't blame them for wanting someone more suited to that type of music. The Thunderbeats carried on for a time with a new lead singer and although I didn't know it at the time, it turned out to be a blessing for me as well.

Chapter Five: Signing David Bowie

In the late 1950s, the top group in South London was The Wranglers. Like so many others, they would mimic The Shadow, both in terms of their sound and even their look. One day I saw an advertisement in the New Musical Express, as it was commonly known at the time before just becoming the NME. The Wranglers were auditioning for a new singer and I thought I had nothing to lose if I went along and tried out. It hadn't gone very well with The Thunderbeats but I could have no complaints as we just didn't suit each other and I still had a lot to learn. I remained convinced that I could still make it in the music world and that fronting a band still offered me the best chance to make that dream come true. Buoyed by the innocence of youth, I went to the audition, only to find it was packed out with hopeful singers. The Wranglers were so popular that everyone wanted to sing with them. Fate had decreed that I would be the last one in a long line of hopefuls, my turn coming long into the evening.

I didn't really look at it as my big break, I think I was still naïve and just didn't know what to expect. It meant I was neither nervous nor really excited. The one thing I was certain about was what song I was going to sing. I had stumbled across a black singer called Ray Charles one day in that Charing Cross Road record shop. Amazing as it seems now, I had never heard of him before and had no idea what type of music he played. But, as before, I liked the cover so I took a chance and bought it. Once again, I was blown away and one of my favourite songs from the album was What I Say.

I thought it might suit my voice so I decided to sing that at the audition. It was a bit of a risk as I don't think many people had heard of either the song or the singer. But I gave it my all and produced what was, at that time, my best performance when I needed it most. The Wranglers might have sounded more like The Shadows but they loved it. They told me I was the best person at the audition and it was largely because they had never heard anything like it. The band's drummer was particularly keen on hiring me and I think it was him more than anything that convinced the others to give me a shot. It was ironic because he left soon after and was replaced by John Aldrick who would also become a good friend and designed a cover of one of my singles when I went solo.

Joining The Wranglers was not without its problems though. The main voice in the band was a chap called Trevor West who played rhythm guitar while his mother financed the group. They weren't keen on me at all as they wanted their frontman to be like Cliff Richard—and you couldn't get more different than me and Cliff. The rest of the boys liked me but I can remember Trevor saying that it wouldn't work and that the girls wouldn't scream at me. He was big on Cliff at the time and wanted The Wranglers to be just like The Shadows. That was understandable, I guess. Cliff and his Shadows were one of the biggest bands around at the time and it was obvious others would try and recreate some of that success. But I had come along and was completely different to what Trevor was looking for. It took some time to get used too.

There was also the not-too-small problem that I wasn't a very good frontman at the start. We started doing a few Cliff Richard songs and it didn't suit me at all. It wasn't my type of music and it didn't suit my voice. The band wanted me to sing like Cliff and I gave it a go, but anyone who has ever seen me perform knows that we are completely poles apart.

We did get some breaks though and even some airplay. There was a show on BBC2 called The Beat Room which we auditioned for along with The Zeffers and the producer picked us to perform. We opened with Bye, Bye Jonny which the producers said was a great opening even though I obviously thought it was more suited to the end of the show.

Although there was no audience, these types of shows went out live and it was all done in a studio. It was nothing like the kind of thing Top of the Pops started doing ten years after. When it was screened, we got a bit of work from it and we went to Scotland and did some more shows for television. I didn't mind singing live and it never really occurred to me that people were watching me in their living rooms. I was never nervous, I just enjoyed singing.

But I was still learning my craft and some of my performances were getting criticised in the likes of the NME. The band was still getting good write-ups, but the press was still unconvinced by me. Trevor couldn't wait to gloat about it as soon as I turned up for rehearsals. He never really warmed to me, even when the Wranglers were at their height and the talk of the West End. He wanted The Shadows and I was James Brown. And this was not me being paranoid. He used to drive us to his gigs in his van and after performing, Trevor would then take us home, one by one.

I was living in Sydenham at the time and would often be the last one on the route. Once or twice, as soon as Trevor had taken home everyone else, he'd drop me off in the middle of Catford—about five or six miles away—and make me walk home. He claimed that he was in a hurry or some nonsense but I knew the real reason was that he just didn't like me and would be happier with me leaving the band.

The writing was on the wall for me as the lead singer of The Wranglers and Trevor seized his chance when I had to go into hospital for a small operation. When I came out, I bought a copy of the NME and there was an advertisement for a gig by Verne Brandon and The Wranglers. To say I was more than a little bit annoyed was an understatement. It was one thing wanting me out because I didn't look or sound like Cliff Richard, but to do it in such an underhand way was a really dirty trick.

A few weeks later, the bass player found me and looked to smooth things over, telling me it wasn't working with Verne and that they wanted me back. Ironically, it all changed when the band played in the interval of Cliff

Richard's film, the Young Ones. It was here we finally started getting noticed.

At that time, it was common practice for a big film to have an interlude and this was usually filled with some live music on stage. We had been booked to play the Plaza Cinema in Catford and I sang Shout as well as a Brook Benton Song called So Many Ways and You Can't Judge A Book By The Cover by Bo Diddley. I thought this last song was particularly apt as a black man fronting a white band was so different to everything else out there at the time. I can remember us walking off stage and the manager of the Plaza coming up to me and telling me I had real stage presence and personality when I sang. It was nice to hear that, even if it would be a long time before I believed any compliments directed towards me.

The band was slowly changing its attitude to music. That was always what I wanted to happen and I was aided by our new keyboard player, Alan Reeves, who was also a fan of my kind of music. When he joined, everything started to change and I immediately felt more comfortable, if not completely confident, as a frontman. I used to go round Alan's house virtually every night to practice and it was no coincidence that the band's fortunes also changed and we became more and more popular.

We played a number of venues across South London including Lewisham Town Hall, the Savoy Rooms and the Golden Slipper Ballroom before extending ourselves across the British Isles where we would regularly perform four nights a week. With the reviews getting better and me settling into the band nicely, the logical step was to turn professional and we even featured in the local newspapers after signing a deal under the EMI label.

The cutting described as a rhythm and blues band and even gave our exact home addresses, something you couldn't imagine in the papers these days. Our fans learnt that leads guitarist Tony Denton's likes were "going to bed early and having my hair cut". Not exactly rock 'n' roll was our Tony. The article also told the world that our equipment included a van for travelling which was valued at several thousands of pounds. A helpful piece of information for any would-be burglar.

Slowly changing from a skittle band to one that played rhythm and blues meant we were always on the lookout for new sounds. And I knew just where to look as Charing Cross Road once again proved a valuable source of inspiration. One time I went in there and saw this album by someone called James Brown and the Famous Flames. I had never heard of James Brown or any of his songs but the cover caught my eye so I bought it and took it home. The album was James Brown live at the Apollo and it was simply fantastic. I really wanted the band to perform some of the songs and to my surprise, they really liked it. Well almost. Trevor and his Mum were once again the ones who needed most convincing.

Fortunately, they were out-voted and we set about trying to make it work. The band decided we needed some brass and we put an advert in the NME. But I already knew just the man—a musician I had met by chance who would go on to have success spanning five decades and sell well over 130 million albums.

Getting to the record shop in Charing Cross Road would always mean grabbing a train to and from Sydenham. I would do this most Fridays and one afternoon I was standing on the platform waiting for my train home when I saw this bloke next to me. In those days, everyone was wearing Italian high heels and flares. But this chap had tight jeans tucked into his boots and a suede jacket with frills hanging down. He might have looked a little strange to some, but he wore it well, complemented by his hair which was combed like Elvis. A little bored waiting for the train, I decided to talk to this interesting-looking man and we hit it off. He introduced himself as David Jones, unbeknown to me he would later change this to David Bowie. At that time, he was living in Bromley, not far from me, and I would often see him at the end of the week waiting for a train.

In the end, we had about ten people respond to our NME advert for brass and David was one of them. Like with my own audition, he was the last one to play. He was an accomplished saxophonist and he was comfortably the best we heard on the day. In addition, we wanted someone with a growl when he played and David certainly had that. So for about three gigs and about two to three weeks, here I was playing with the future Ziggy Stardust, a man who ranks among the ten best selling pop artists in UK history. Its strange thinking about that now as David was just a member of the band, no airs or graces. He got on with everyone and he seemed to enjoy it, but unfortunately he didn't stick around too long. He did give me one pearl of wisdom before he left the band, something that I have never forgotten to this day. Before he left, he told me: "Ken you are good you know, but if you want to be successful, you need to write your own songs." He was right, of course, and it is nice thinking back that someone like David Bowie had confidence in me. But he was also smart and knew The Wranglers would never make money playing cover songs all the time. A little while later he wrote Space Oddity and then became Ziggy Stardust and the rest was history. Despite his fame and fortune as the king of glam rock, something didn't sit well with me. I felt he wasn't being himself. When I knew him, he would talk about his love of soul music and this showed in the way he would play sax. I know he once recorded Midnight Hour by Wilson Pickett. My one regret is we never thought to take a photo of David while he was in the band, but then why would we think we would need one?

When I first got into showbusiness, some people told me that there was no racism. But there was a lot behind the scenes, and some radio stations wouldn't even play my songs. But this wasn't just confined to The Wranglers. Even the Rolling Stones had this problem when they were starting out as they thought Mick Jagger sounded too black. Radio Luxembourg was one that did, but it would come on late at night and the reception was terrible.

And it certainly wasn't just the radio. Due to my colour or maybe because it was a black person fronting a white band, the newspaper editors were nervy or something. They would use a picture of the band but, where possible, cut me out. This wasn't the days of Photoshop so they would hope that it would be a picture where I was at the end of the band, so I could easily be cropped. The people at the paper tried to almost laugh it off by saying there was no room for a wider photo. But I knew what was going on and the band knew what was going on, but we never talked about it and I never complained. It seemed simpler not to rock the boat, not when things were going so well with The Wranglers. Should I have done more to complain? Maybe. But I wasn't one to make a fuss and I didn't want to create any problems for my band members. If that meant that I sometimes wasn't in a photo in the local paper because of some ill-advised editor, so be it. I could live with that.

Doreen and I would have quite a giggle when we saw it in the newspapers. But for our fans, it was a very different story. They would contact the newspaper and ask why I wasn't in the photo and often give the journalist or editor a hard time about it. That was more important to me than any little article.

My first song as a soloist was Liza Jane, which was ironically the same name as the Wranglers first record. Ours was completely different and didn't suit me at all. It was a bad song for me but it was great for the band as it had a fantastic instrumental section with some amazing guitar work. Despite this, our manager at the time set us up with a fantastic photo shoot to go with our first song. We were sent to the top of the EMI building, whose label the record was under, and pictures of the band were taken. It was great fun and just gave me another taster of what I wanted to do with my life.

We toured for several months, getting a name for ourselves even if Liza Jane didn't have the chart success we had hoped for. We had appeared on the television show Thank Your Lucky Stars and we thought it was time to release our second record, Somebody Help Me. We had decided to donate all our royalties to Oxfam, a move that was quite uncommon at the time. It attracted the interest of the newspapers and one described us as "the local group that made good" after we returned to South London to perform at the Eltham Baths.

When the records came out, I would always make sure I would send one to my Nan in Trinidad. She told me that she played Liza Jane everyday proudly telling everyone that it was her grandson singing on the song. She was obviously biased but it was still a nice thing to hear.

Little did she, or I, know that bigger things were coming for The Wranglers. Starting with a date with the silver screen.

Chapter Six: Who Doesn't Want To Be In A Film?

As The Wranglers' success grew, so too did the opportunities. We were young and enjoying our new-found fame and when the chance to star in an actual movie came along, we were never going to turn it down.

Since turning professional, we had taken on a new manager, signing with Harold Shampan, although Trevor's mother was still in the background. One of Harold's many businesses was with the Rank Organisation's Film Music division which produced low-budget musical movies.

It was one of these that he wanted The Wranglers to audition for. Be My Guest was about a band's demo record that got stolen. We were up for a small cameo as a band playing in a talent contest later in the film. Best of all, it was to star Jerry Lee Lewis. For Trevor, this was particularly exciting as the man who sang Great Balls Of Fire was a particular idol for our rhythm guitarist. Not only did we love the idea of being in a film, but if we are able to play one of our own songs during the movie, it would be another great way to showcase what we could do.

Not that you would think I was excited by the opportunity looking at me when we arrived in Harold's office for the audition. I might have looked miserable, and Harold was quick to tell me so, but I was just terribly nervous. I was still learning my trade as a singer and if I had any kind of comfort zone as a performer, auditioning for a part in a film was as far removed from it as you could get.

Although he had recently become our manager, Howard had pre-warned us that there were no guarantees. The band played an instrumental at first and Howard later told me he was fairly unimpressed. Then I started singing Road Runner, by Bo Diddley, and he said it made all the difference. He was looking for a different sound to the other bands who would feature in the film and he had found it.

I was ecstatic. I really wanted to sing in this movie, I mean who doesn't want to be in a film. I knew it could be a good showcase for me and the band and it could lead to exciting times. There was one problem though. Unbeknown to the rest of the band, Howard had taken me to one side and told me that he wanted the camera to focus heavily on me and not on the other members.

This was all I needed. It had taken me a long time to overcome the doubters from within the band and now this golden opportunity to be in the film could risk further division in our ranks. Perhaps naively, and not really thinking about the possible repercussions, I said I didn't mind and the next thing we knew we were at Pinewood Studios.

Despite the Hertfordshire location, Be My Guest was meant to be set in Brighton and featured some really cool classic cars such as Zeffers, Anglias and little Austins and Lambrettas. The big stars in the film were

David Hemmings, Steve Marriott, who would later give up acting and front the Small Faces, Lionel Blair's sister Joyce and of course Jerry Lee Lewis. There were other bands in the film, the likes of the Nashville Teens, and we got a mention in the credits and on the promotional advertising as well. But to be honest, the thought of being in the same film as Jerry Lee Lewis, who at that time was in the peak of his career, was enough for us all.

We didn't get to see the rock 'n' roll legend much as he only had a small bit in the film, like us. But one day we had been filming for most of it when in walked Jerry Lee Lewis himself, not to mention about 20 people with him. It was certainly some entourage. He went to the piano and was filmed and afterwards, of course, everyone crowded round to get his autograph.

I went over to him and started talking to him about Elvis Presley as I knew he had signed to the same label as the King. It seems a bit cheeky to ask a music legend about someone else, but he didn't mind talking about Elvis at all. He was a funny guy and there he was sitting at this piano talking about Elvis Presley. It was amazing and so interesting. I can remember him talking about how many southerners in America didn't like Elvis' songs and called them "devil music". This upset and worried Elvis who one day asked Jerry Lee Lewis if what he was singing was in fact "devil music". Jerry just looked at the King and said 'Elvis, you are the devil'. In the end, Jerry Lee Lewis' song in the film was never officially released giving the film another reason for its cult status.

As for our part, it went largely without any problems. Luckily, I come alive when I'm singing and I quickly threw off any shackles of nervousness. I knew I would. I often used to appear quite edgy or a bit quiet before performing but it was just nerves. As soon as I got on stage, I transformed.

A couple of months later, Be My Guest was released in the cinema as a B film to support the main feature, Morecambe and Wise's The Intelligence Man. This was quite common place at the time in cinemas with B films often low-budget and shown before the more illustrious main film. For us, we didn't care if it was A, B or any other letter of the alphabet. Our moment of fame had arrived. In the end, it wasn't 15 minutes of fame, more like about three minutes shortly after the hour mark. But I was still immensely proud. We looked good and more importantly sounded good as we sang Somebody Stop Me under the guise of Rocky Steele and the Sparks.

I guess I knew at the time that the film wasn't exactly going to win an Oscar but for a while, I got a little big-headed about it all. For a short while, I'm embarrassed to admit, I did think I was a star, it was probably the only time in my life I had something of an ego. I can remember going to the cinema and seeing it on the big screen and for a while I thought I had made it, however brief my appearance. I was quickly brought back down to earth though. Doreen wasn't too fussed about it and my Mum and Dad didn't even go to the cinema to watch it.

I was paid £60 for my bit-part and I went straight out and spent the lot on a really nice silk silver suit. I was really pleased as that was a fair amount of money at that time and it was nice being able to walk into a fashionable clothes story and purchase exactly what I wanted. Naturally, any fame from the film lasted about as long as the money and I soon realised that I was never going to be a big movie star. If I was unsure about the film when it came out, time has done it no great favours since. It hasn't aged well, in fact it is a pretty second-rate film.

But despite its low quality, Be My Guest was actually regarded as a big thing at the time for Howard and his Film Music division. And since then, it has achieved something of a cult following. I think it has a certain coolness to it, given the decade it was made in and the classic cars on show. It epitomises the swinging sixties away from London and there are some cool cars and cool tunes in it.

It is occasionally on one of the SKY film channels and I guess that is something to tell the grandchildren. I knew at the time that it was pretty awful, but this doesn't stop us all from thinking we were stars. It was a nice experience. I have had friends come back from a holiday in Spain or Germany and say they heard me singing on the television on Be My Guest. One person wrote that the film has a bad plot and bad acting, but was still a cool film. I'm more than happy with that.

This wasn't actually the end of The Wranglers' brush with the film world. Our song, Who Do You Think I

Am, was actually featured playing in the background in a film called The Pleasure Girls a year after Be My Guest. But to this day, I have never seen it nor had a penny from royalties. I only found out about it years later when Doreen's sister watched it by chance and said she thought it sounded like me. I'm sure someone, somewhere made some money out of it.

Chapter Seven: London In The Sixties

Be My Guest had done exactly what we had hoped. Our profile had never been greater and the bookings were flooding in.

We may have only had a cameo role in the film but it seemed that even a few minutes screen time could be as effective as a number of gigs across the country.

That said, we never underestimated the importance of publicity in any way, shape or form.

We were getting a good name for ourselves and getting good coverage in the London Evening News and the Evening Standard. In those days you wouldn't be successful unless you got good press and good airtime on the radio.

But this wasn't without its problems. During the height of our fame, a chap called David Lands, who would later work with me on my solo record Nothing Can Change, decided to put a small photo of me on the front of a magazine aimed at teenage girls. He knew I was getting a name for myself and thought I would be ideal for the cover. But I was told he was later hauled into the office of the editor who demanded answers over why a black man had appeared on the front of his magazine. David almost lost his job over the incident.

It was incredibly rare for a black musician to have his photo in the paper during the early part of the 1960s, but here was I coming along and getting exposure on almost a weekly basis. Some editors didn't like it, others didn't know how to cope with it.

Despite the good coverage of both me and the band, we were never going to rest on our laurels. Every single member of The Wranglers was hard-working, knowing that we could never simply think we had made it.

Especially, as we still yearned for that big hit. I thought I had found the perfect song which would propel us to stardom when one day at that record shop in Charing Cross Road, I stumbled across Shout by the Isley Brothers. I hadn't heard the song before but as soon as I played it I just knew it was destined to be a hit.

We were still under the management of Harold Shampan so I rushed it to him eagerly waiting for him to get us in the studio right away. Unfortunately, he didn't share my enthusiasm. He described it as 'jungle music' and said it wouldn't suit the band. We were pushing boundaries with our sound but Howard felt this was a step too far and that the music-loving public was not ready for it. A few years later, they must have obviously adapted their likes when a 15-year-old Lulu brought it out and turned it into a hit record.

It wasn't long after that Harold and The Wranglers parted company. I think some of the band members thought they were not getting enough exposure and that it was all getting a bit too much about me. I think this is a common problem with lead singers who are, right or wrong, seen as the figurehead of a band or group. I think we could have handled our departure with Harold a little better and he had some good contacts with Radio London which we lost when we split up. Harold tried to convince me to leave the band and become a top solo cabaret artist. I probably would have earned more money down this route but I craved a top-selling record and I still firmly believed that it was going to happen with The Wranglers.

Amid all the changes going on in the background, we were becoming more and more popular and with it, my confidence was finally starting to grow. I never thought I was a big star, even though some people thought I was big-headed, mistaking it for confidence on stage. But I was starting to feel more confident on stage, having more belief in my voice and what I brought to the band. It had all come together and I was loving every minute of it.

I always found if I was nervous before a performance, then it would generally go well. I was never a cocky person anyway, but I think if I had started getting above my station, I would put on a bad show. Even though I think I am a more confident performer now, I still get nervous. I could be playing at somewhere I have been dozens of times before but the nerves still kick in just before I go on stage. Fortunately, I know how to handle it better now and I don't let it worry me. I know that I am myself on stage and if people don't like me, there is little I can do about that. I feel I have nothing left to prove.

The Wranglers hadn't gone unnoticed and for a time I was getting head-hunted to join other bands. The

Ram Jam Band, formed by Peter Gage, was one who seemed particularly keen on me joining but I always felt that I would have had little artistic influence on the direction of the band. It had taken me a long while to convince The Wranglers that we should try different sounds and I certainly didn't want to start all over again

And there was little reason to leave a band that was becoming popular all over the place. We followed Sammy Davis Jr into the Pigalle in the West End but the place where we made our name was the Ad Lib in Leicester Square. Anybody who was anybody was there. All the big stars would come and watch us and they would say positive things about me and the band.

We were only booked for a short tour at the Ad Lib but when we left, the owners actually found the numbers started to dwindle so we soon came back for more shows.

It was at the club that I first encountered the enchanting Dionne Warwick. It was during one of her first visits to the country and we had a nice chat and she said she wanted to take us all back to America. While perhaps she wasn't as well-known as she is now, it still gave us a great thrill and we thought about it long and hard. But we decided not to leave England because we felt we would be paired with someone like Bobby Rydell or Paul Anca on tour and that wasn't our scene. We only wanted to try and break the States if we could take a hit record with us. The Beatles said the same thing but of course they went on to have hit after hit. Even now, I still think it was a smart move of ours and it certainly didn't affect our popularity in the capital.

Another night we had Petula Clark in the audience but I have to say that was a slightly odd experience. I wasn't a bad looking man in my youth, even if I do say so myself, and I would often get attention from girls. Being a singer in a band was of course another reason. I was going steady with Doreen, but it didn't stop certain girls approaching me and trying to flirt with me, even though I wasn't having any of it.

On this particular night, a woman who was by then an international superstar was sitting in the audience and simply couldn't take her eyes off me. Petula was just staring at me, without a care of who might spot her. Thinking back, it was quite flattering but at the time it was actually a little off-putting. I didn't think it was best to tell Doreen about that particular brush with a celebrity.

Other attention was a lot more welcome. Buddy Greco, another member of the legendary Rat Pack, was a fan and used to see us play quite a lot. He would call me over to his table and tell me how my voice made him feel homesick. It was one of the nicest things anyone has ever said about my singing. I can remember years later when I was out of London, hearing Buddy being interviewed by Michael Parkinson and recalling those kind words he uttered to me more than 30 years before.

Buddy was actually quoted in the London Evening Standard as saying he was convinced he was listening to Sammy Davis and that I was 'more like Sammy than Sammy is'. To top it off, the headline of the article stated: "Sammy Davis comes from Lewisham". I was blown away. To be compared to a great like Sammy Davis Jr was something else, more than I could have ever possibly imagined.

Ironically, it would not be my only association with the great man, even if the time our paths actually crossed did not go so well.

One of our best shows was at the Playboy Club in Mayfair where all the famous faces would turn up. Sammy Davis had come over to do the Talk of the Town and was staying in the penthouse of the Playboy Club while I was singing in the discotheque below. My act would always start with the band doing an instrumental opening and then I would come on and say a few words. So one evening, the band started and as I walked on to the stage I noticed Sammy Davis Jr dancing on the floor with a woman.

It was very exciting seeing a hero of mine as I prepared to sing. But I have to admit that I got a little overexcited by the sight of such a legend on the dancefloor so I called his name out over the microphone. Though it was meant as a compliment and a welcome, this was a big no-no at any of the top London clubs. These stars never wanted the spotlight on them, they were just there to relax and have a good time. As soon as I had said his name out loud across the Playboy Club, he and his lady friend moved straight from the dance floor and went and sat down in a private booth.

To be honest, I thought nothing of it at the time. But when I finished my act, the manager of the club came up to me and read me the riot act over what I had done. He told me in no uncertain terms to never call out anyone's name again as they had "just come for a quiet drink". It certainly put me in my place and I realised instantly what I had done and why it had been so frowned upon. But just in case I hadn't, Sammy Davis had something up his sleeve to make me realise who was boss.

As before, the band played me on for the second act but as I walked on past where Sammy Davis was sitting, they got up and walked out. They were clearly annoyed and Sammy had left it to the perfect moment, when I was just about to sing, to make it plain and clear what he thought. They had killed me and my act that night stone dead. I knew what I did was wrong. I had been warned at the Ad Lib that these celebrities want to come for a quiet drink and not be disturbed. I had done it before when Nancy Wilson came to the Ad Lib. She was a really good jazz singer and would play a lot of gigs in Vegas.

But that was not the end of my dealings with Sammy Davis Jnr. A couple of evening afterwards, purely by chance, I was coming up the stairs and Sammy was coming down. We were passing each other when he said: "Kenny, I hope we taught you a lesson the other night. We didn't want to do it but you know why we did. We know the manager had a go at you and I am sorry we did it that way. But you had to learn a lesson." Randomly, he then asked me if I wanted a drink and I ended up talking with this world famous singer who I had offended just a few nights before. He didn't talk much and he seemed really nervous about going on stage. He had a black coat with the collar up and a hat on, so you could barely see his face. It was nice to have a drink with him and to clear the air. It was a simple lesson really. He wanted to stay anonymous and stay in the shadows when he was in the club. I can understand that.

While The Wranglers' popularity continued to grow, we couldn't always say the same about the money. We were getting paid about £20 a gig and £12 wages so it was okay, but still not a great amount. I always insisted that every band member got paid the same even if, as lead singer, I could have privately got paid more. That's why it always hurt a little when certain members of the band thought I was getting too much of the limelight.

But the lack of both money and a hit record wasn't everything. All things considered, it was great being in and around London in those days. There was such a special atmosphere and the music coming along was so fresh and so different. Elvis Presley and The Beatles played a big part in that of course. They were both inspirational to me and The Wranglers and to so many people in showbusiness at that time. The clubs were really alive and it was great to be singing in them.

I didn't feel like I was a huge star but looking back, I was in one sense lucky to be playing in the likes of the Ad Lib and the Playboy clubs.

The Ad Lib was a particular favourite. It was a hive of activity and atmosphere. All the main players in the business, all the big stars, went there and for a time, they were listening to me.

We also got to play a half-hour set in the London Palladium. This was perhaps more common than it is now, but it was still an amazing venue and a real privilege for us. Sammy Davis and Judy Garland had performed there so for us to follow in those footsteps was a real career highlight.

There still remained a pocket of people who would run us down and say I couldn't sing. Perhaps that is why we didn't know how good we were. Why did they run us down? Now, thinking back, it might have been jealousy over the band's success. It might have been the fact they didn't like a black person fronting a white band or the fact that it was working so well.

We released further songs, The Tracker and Moonshine to name but two, but I think there was a feeling that if we were going to have a hit record, it would have been with one of our first releases or straight after Be My Guest. When that didn't happen, I think certain members of the band started to lose a little heart and change their priorities and I can completely understand that.

Trevor and his mother were predictably the first to leave but the writing was on the wall even before that. Our base guitarist, Colin McKay, decided to pack in the touring game and settle down and I think he was quick to see that the end was coming. We had run our path, The Wranglers were no more.

People ask me why it was that we never quite broke through and to this day I don't think there is one single reason. Maybe we were a little naïve in places, maybe our managers didn't make the right choices, maybe we were just not in the right place at the right time.

I think we were not helped by the fact that I was a black man in a white band. It scared managers, promoters, labels who were all simply not willing to take a chance and stump up some cash to support us. There are parts of me that can understand this, but I also think it lacked foresight and most of all guts.

In general, there was still this reluctance to invest in a black artist. This is not me being paranoid, far from it, as I used to be told this to my face. The record producers would say it would be difficult to get a black artist off the ground. They would tell me straight and they wouldn't care if it hurt my feelings which it would invariably do. You had Emile Ford, the West Indian singer, in the 1950s and Kenny Lynch a decade later but the majority of black artists had little chance of success at that time.

The Wranglers were popular in the West End and I truly believe we could have had a hit record, but it was not to be. I think another reason was the music we were playing at the time was deemed too risky to some or "jungle music" to quote a former manager. I suppose I was partly to blame for that. The band had realised and appreciated my talents to an extent that we were playing songs by the likes of James Brown and Ray Charles. The downside of this is that these great men were still little known. Without meaning to sound big-headed, I think we were a little ahead of our time. The sounds of the time consisted more of The Shadows, that is where Trevor certainly had a point.

I remember reading that Bill Wyman went through a similar problem when he did blues music but the Rolling Stones stuck at it and look what happened.

But I don't want to sound like a victim. When I listen to interviews of even the most famous black stars, they all went through what I went through. For instance, Eartha Kitt had her trials and tribulations when she married white real estate man William McDonald. You have to choose how you are going to deal with it. You can either react which is probably what some people want and actually expect or you can take the high road and just get on with your life. I certainly wasn't going to let some moronic comments cause any problems, both personally and professionally. You just have to get through it, often turning a blind eye to what has been said. No matter what, I have always tried to go through life with a smile on my face.

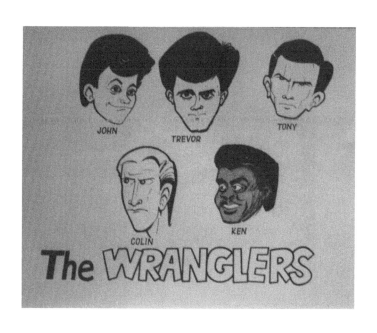

Now turning professional

ive local boys—The Wranglers—who will have reached yet another mile-
one in their careers in June when their first record will be released.

ee pop group, whose leader
r-old Trevor West, of 2
orook-rd., made his first
, are turning professional
heir first disc due for re-
n June.

n E.M.I. label and under
me of 'The Wranglers', the
ill be cutting their debut
a recording session for
on May 12.

list of the group — who
rhythm and Blues music
-year-old Kenny Bernard,
Holmshaw-rd., Sydenham.
at Fernando, Trinidad,
joined the group about
onths ago and names his
te recording artistes as
arles, Andy Williams and
Richard.

group includes 22-year-
y Denton (lead guitarist,
iea player and vocalist)

dislikes are "going to bed early
and having my hair cut."

Then there are Colin Black
(bass guitar), aged 21, of 81
King Alfred Avenue, Bellingham,
who was born in Scotland — he
lists Ricky Nelson and Julie
London as his favourite performers and also likes "veteran
cars," and John Lee Aldrick
(drums), aged 23, of 2 Athelney
Street, Bellingham, who likes
the work of Chuck Berry and
Bo Diddley — his hobby is car-
toon drawing.

Trevor, who also chose the
name for the group, plays rhythm guitar, prefers horror films
and likes the work of Jerry Lee
Lewis.

They have been managed for
the past two years by Mrs.
Brown, Trevor's mother, who
tells me that they usually hold

terested in music," she added
"they played mostly skiffle numbers Now their sound has chan
ged and they play rhythm numbers and the Blues."

With ever increasing fans an
followers, 'The Wranglers' hav
been working regularly fou
nights a week in dance halls an
theatres all over the Britis
Isles.

Naming the numerous hal
in which they have played
the borough, Mrs. Brown me
tioned the ABC Cinema, Catfor
Lewisham Town Hall, the Savi
Rooms and the Golden Slipp
Ballroom.

Performing at a YMCA club
Woolwich recently, they were
troduced to Lord Snowdi
Princess Margaret's husbai
who was visiting the premise

Chapter Eight: My Best Chance Of A Hit

I had a simple choice to make. Going solo after three great years fronting The Wranglers or leave music behind altogether?

Of course there wasn't really any choice even if going on stage on my own was a big shock to the system.

A part of me felt like I was starting again, that I had to prove myself all over. Never blessed with the greatest of confidence, I suddenly found I lost a lot of the bravado that had built up inside me as The Wranglers made their name. I wasn't at a stage when I could ignore all the doubters and now I would have to face them on my own. Becoming a solo artist was certainly a lonely place at first.

I never wanted The Wranglers to split up. But as soon as the various band members started to settle down, it was inevitable and understandable. And perhaps, if we were going to make it, it was always going to be in those first couple of great years together. Indeed had we achieved fame and fortune, I doubt whether the various people would have left the band.

But once they did, there was no chance for the band. Replacing them was never an option so, as I say, I had to go it alone which invariably meant learning all over again.

I quickly realised that I liked the support of band members on a stage and that The Wranglers had been some kind of security blanket to me. I'm not afraid to admit it was more intimidating going solo.

I had a new record producer, Mervyn Conn, who would later make his name putting on the International Festivals of Country Music at Wembley Arena for more than 20 years. To be fair to Mervyn, he put more money behind me than anyone else in my career. My first record as a solo artist was What Love Brings and I couldn't accuse Mervyn of not supporting me on it.

We recorded inside the studios of Pye Records with a live orchestra which was an incredible buzz. I wasn't nervous playing with the orchestra as it was more excitement than anything. It certainly gave me an extra edge knowing that everyone was watching me, waiting for me to lead and wanting me to be successful. I fed off this positive energy inside the studio and when everything goes well in that type of situation, there is no better feeling for a recording artist. I just went in there and recorded the song. It would be great to just have one more chance to be in a studio with a live band. It is now probably just a pipedream, but at least I got the chance to experience this amazing sensation.

On the other side of What Love Brings was a cover of an old Sam Cooke song called Nothing Can Change This Love. I was mad on the soul legend, ever since I saw him play at the Lewisham Odeon supporting Little Richard. It was the first time I had ever heard Cupid and I still perform that song in my act to this very day. I also liked the way Little Richard got the crowd going and it is something I try to do as well, perhaps not quite in the same energetic style.

For me to record a Sam Cooke number seemed a perfect fit for me and my voice. Understandably given the effort they had put into it, my management were keener on the original song which they thought would have more chance of being successful. My managers published it themselves but, as I thought they would, the public preferred Nothing Can Change This Love.

It received some good airplay, not least on an old Sunday radio show called Family Favourites which was designed to link British families with their loved ones stationed overseas. It was presented by Jean Metcalfe and I think my song struck a chord with servicemen and their families as it was about someone writing a letter to a loved one miles away. One of the lyrics went: "If you go a million miles away, I'll write a letter every day."

What Love Brings got a lot less airtime, although Kenny Everett did sometimes put it on his Radio London show. It's strange because I attracted some criticism at the time over the song, but it became my most popular hit with the Northern Soul contingent some 30 years later.

My next song came so close to giving me the hit record I had craved since my days in Trinidad. I had first encountered the song Hey Joe through David Lands who had nearly lost his job by putting me on the cover of a magazine a few years back. We had remained in touch and I knew that David would often go to Liverpool docks and get all the new records coming in from America off the merchant sailors who had brought them over. This was one of the only ways we could listen to new music as the radio would still play the tried and trusted, but successful, artists.

One such song was Hey Joe, then an unknown record written by Tim Rose, which David thought would be ideal for my voice and could be turned into a massive hit. I couldn't have agreed more with him. When I first heard it, I couldn't contain my excitement about what might lay ahead. It was still a time when rock and roll was king and there was still a heavy emphasis on the performer, whether a soloist or lead singer in a band. Then this guitar-heavy song came out of nowhere and even though it was different, I knew straight away it was going to be a hit.

It was one of the first times I had got really excited about a song and the potential of me recording it and turning it into a hit. But I was a little wary about playing it to Mervyn. I had been down this road before with Shout and Harold. What if Mervyn didn't like it? I had little choice but to play it to him, I had no idea how I would record it otherwise. There was a mixture of nerves and excitement as I knocked on Mervyn's door with this unknown record in my hand. Fortunately, he felt exactly the same way and once again backed up his belief with a little bit of finance. Within 24 hours he had booked a studio with one of the top arrangers at the time, Reg Guest, working on it. Mervyn also got a big orchestra in to record the song at the renowned

Olympic Sound Studios in central London. The studio was the scene for some of the most famous bands of all time. It was here that the Rolling Stones recorded their first single, Come On, and The Troggs' Wild Thing was also recorded. It was also used, ironically, by Jimi Hendrix. And then there was me.

This kind of thing was never thrown at me, the underlying and unsaid message being that we had a hit on our hands. Finally, I thought. There were several factors why this little-known song was going to be massive. It was a different sound to what Britain was experiencing at the time, and different in a good way. It was also more in keeping with the flower-power era that was sweeping the country. And lyrically, it was fantastic. All I had to do was make sure I did it justice when I recorded it. After not making it with The Wranglers, I now possessed a kind of 'if it happens, it happens' mentality when I thought about my chances of a hit record. But even I have to admit that I felt more than a tinge of excitement by this record.

While there had been times when I thought the band had a potential hit on our hands, this was the big one for me. This was the one time when I had complete confidence. In those days, you didn't have to worry so much about copyright as it was often very difficult to find out who wrote the original versions. All you had to do was change just one word and the song was yours. So I was told to change Hey Joe to Hey Woman. I didn't completely agree with this but after the recording session had been paid for along with a top orchestra and arranger, I felt I couldn't really argue about it. In fact, the whole production cost a lot of money. I had about four backing singers for that recording and it all went perfectly. So much so, that I did the recording in one take. But it didn't just stop there. We even put advertising posters up telling people this song was coming out. This had never happened to me before. It was part surreal, part exciting.

But unfortunately my naivety was to prove my downfall. What happened next has somewhat haunted me ever since. An engineer working at the studio said he really liked what I had done and asked if he could borrow the recording. I stupidly said yes and unbeknown to me he played the recording to his friend, who just so happened to be Chas Chandler, manager of Jimi Hendrix. As I say, with little or no copyright in those days, there was nothing we could do.

We were told that my recording was originally scheduled to break into Radio London's Fab 40, the 1960s version of the Top 40. It was very powerful and actually more popular than the BBC stations. Once you got in there, the radio station would play you three or four times a day and there was every chance you would go up the charts. My management and I were convinced we had a massive hit on our hands with Hey Woman. But unlike nowadays, when you can have different versions of a song in the same charts, that didn't happen then. Jimi recorded Hey Joe and that was put in the Fab 40 instead. My Hey Woman was blown out of the water. The rest is history.

It sounds farcical and unbelievable, but if I'd had a slightly more sensible head and not been suckered in so much, I could have recorded something that became one of the most iconic songs of all time. It upset me at the time as it was a little underhand. But that happened in the music business quite a lot and I didn't whine about It. You just had to get on with it rather than think about what might have been. It was a very different song to what was around at the time and I think that is why it appealed to Jimi so much. And with such a heavy emphasis on guitar, it really suited him and his talents so I couldn't really complain.

It was just another example as to why you should record your own songs. I tried this once or twice, writing a little with Peter Gage, but it wasn't really where my talents lied. As well as Mervyn, I had Hal Ashley and Howard Sinclair working with me. They were financially supported by a man called Seftan Myers who was friends were Bernard Delfonte, the man behind the biggest agency in the world at that time. You would have thought with all these people combined, somebody would stump up some cash to give me a chance to break through. But sadly no. I continued to get good gigs in the West End, and good compliments, but that bit of luck, or maybe that bit of financial backing, sadly eluded me. Only Mervyn, at times, took a punt on me and I thank him for that. Some people would probably say that I lacked that certain something to make it big, that it had nothing to do with financial backing. They are entitled to that opinion.

Hal and Howard once arranged for Bernard Delfont to come and see me perform at the Celebrity. Bernard had converted the London Hippodrome into the Talk of the Town restaurant attracting the likes of Frank Sinatra and Shirley Bassey. He had seen my face all over the papers and he wanted to come and see for himself what all the fuss was about. I wanted to show Bernard the real me and had planned to sing Shout. But Hal and Howard convinced me that this particular club owner wouldn't like it so I sang a safer number by Frank Sinatra. It was a big mistake. I should have done my own regular material or at least put my own take on a song rather than mimic legends like Sinatra or Nat King Cole. I trusted my managers and their judgement but I was left singing songs that simply didn't suit me. Rather than impress Bernard Delfonte, he probably left thinking I was no different than any other club singer.

Howard Sinclair was a very good businessman but he seemed to me to know very little about showbusiness. He was all about making as much money as possible rather than investing time and energy for greater long-term goals. I suppose I can understand that, but to be in the centre of that kind of thinking was incredibly frustrating when all I wanted was the right of level support which would have then led to a record contract. Unfortunately, I was too naïve to see what was happening when really I should have moved on elsewhere.

In the end I parted company with Seftan Myers and went on my own. As a parting gift, or perhaps a golden handshake, he paid up what was owed on my first ever car, a brand new Austin 1100. There was still about £700 owing so it was a generous thing to do.

I always had problems with the people tasked to help me. There was a lot of interest in producing my songs but my managers were always asking for too much money. Whether they were simply being greedy or holding out for what they thought I was worth, only they will know. Unfortunately at that time, it was the managers rather than the performers who held all the power.

One song I had to wait to record was A Change Is Gonna Come by Sam Cooke. I used to perform it when I was singing in the Best Seller club, next to what is now the big Odeon cinema in the West End where they have all the film premiers. One night, a man came over and said he really liked my version and that I should record it. The only problem was that it was at a time when racial tensions across the world were at boiling point and the meaning of the song wouldn't go down well with everyone.

Unsurprisingly, certain sections of the media were keen for me to record it. I had more than one newspaper tell me that if I did release it, they would ensure that I got a lot of coverage in their pages. Whether it would be the right kind of coverage or simply a way of stirring up racial tensions, I guess we will never know. My record company, Pye, at the time were very nervy about me recording it, but eventually Mervyn gave it the green light and we put it on a B side. The song eventually became famous when Barack Obama was elected US President and Seal released a cover version of it.

One of the problems when I left The Wranglers was that I got myself involved with some bad managers. There was some who obviously knew the music industry but they were never willing to fully back me, whether in effort or finance. Without any money behind me to promote me, I became nothing more than a decent club singer and my chances of recording a hit weakened by the year.

Of course, I have to take a fair share of the blame for this. I was a little naïve in choosing who to go with and allowing myself to be taken in by some smart-talking people.

Having a good manager would have made all the difference at the time. It was part of the reason why the Rolling Stones became so successful.

Chapter Nine: Missed Opportunities

If my brush with The Jimi Hendrix Experience wasn't enough, I also missed out on potentially recording other songs that went on to become massive hits for other people. It became an unfortunate theme of my singing career in London.

One such time actually came when I wasn't making much money at all from music. I was still living with Mum and Dad who supported me in the fantastic way parents do. But in the end I know I had to get a regular job, not least because Doreen had broken her leg after she was hit by a car. I found work at the Morphy Richards electrical company. It was pretty much worlds away from what I wanted to do and I never enjoyed it. But we needed the money and it ticked that box. I nearly found the perfect escape route only for my management to scupper my dreams.

One night after getting home from work, a little fed up and unhappy with my lot, my Mum said I had a phone call from a man called Tony McAuley. She seemed unfazed by it but I knew Tony was a song writer from Denmark Street. He would also later become the manager of Irish singer Enya. But I was so disillusioned with my factory job and the fact that my music career had literally stalled, that at first I didn't even bother to ring him back. I didn't mean to appear rude, it was just that I was down at the time and not thinking straight.

Eventually, I saw sense and called him a few weeks later. But it was a few weeks too late. He said he did have a song for me, but that I had missed the boat. It was a song called Baby Now That I Found You but he had given it to a band called The Temptations who would go on to have tens of millions of albums sold.

Amazingly it wasn't my only missed opportunity. I was also offered a chance to record Born Free, written by the legendary John Barry. One night at the Best Seller, a man came in and called me to his table. He told me that he liked the way I sung and that he had a song for me. He asked for my address so he could send it to me and see what I thought. I was always meeting people at the clubs and many were offering me various things, but I never really took any notice. Yet, I gave this man my address in Forest Gate where Doreen and I were living at the time. The first time I heard Born Free, I fell in love with it. The lyrics reminded me of A Change is Gonna Come. The problem came when I took it to my management team. It transpired that they had their own publishing company who they wanted to handle any recordings and releases. But the song belonged to Screen Gems and there was no leeway for negotiation. In the end, Matt Monro sung it and it went on to win an Academy Award for Best Original Song.

This was one of my biggest disappointments in my music career. I had really wanted to record Born Free. I think it would have really suited my voice but I was ultimately left deflated and rejected. I felt that my management team were less keen because they felt they wouldn't make any money out of me recording the song. So there was no way they were going to back me by paying for a big orchestra to really give the song what it was worth. History has of course shown them to be completely wrong. Matt Monroe did a fantastic version and perhaps he was a safer bet than me. But I know I would have done the song justice. It was just another example of how too many men in the industry just wanted to make as much money in the shortest time possible, but didn't know the first thing about how to achieve this.

I was perhaps guilty of listening to my management too much, but that is how it was then. Once I got a chance to spend a day with Screen Gem publishers who put me in a room with wall-to-wall songs on their shelves from all over the world. There was a record player in the corner and they gave me a chance to pick a few to look at possibly releasing. I chose You Don't Have To Say You Love Me and Groovy Kind of Love. Both had not been released yet, they were not even known by anyone. But when I asked a manager at Screen Gem about them, he said that I couldn't have them because I sounded too much like a West Indian. It seems that my voice only applied to just a handful of songs in that impressive room. Disgusted and disgruntled, I quickly made my excuses and left.

But my musical career in the 1960s and 1970s wasn't just about missed opportunities. I also got to mix with some of the biggest stars in the country. I supported The Who in Birmingham which was very daunting. I expected the people who would pay money to watch such a great band would not necessarily be my usual fanbase. But to my surprise, as well as relief, I actually got a great reception. Their manager came up to me and said I went down really well and Pete Townsend said I should have my own band. I was flabbergasted.

I think anyone who has ever shared any time with the band, however brief, has their own stories about Keith Moon. I'm no different. Mine and the band's dressing room were next door to each other. I was chilling out with John Taffe, who had been the guitarist with The Wranglers, when we suddenly heard gunshots next door. Without thinking, I dashed into their dressing room and there was Keith shooting at the ceiling. He was perfectly calm as if this was the actions of a rational man. Completely dumbfounded, I made my excuses, pretending almost not to notice what had just happened, and left. When we got back to the safety of our dressing room, John and I just looked at each other and laughed.

I also played at some great places. Singing at the Playboy Club was exactly like all the stereotypes and myths. A posh and glamorous setting, full of beautiful women and rich men. Even the knives and forks stood out, resplendent with black ivory handles. So much so, I am embarrassed to confess, that I did once or twice take a couple home. I saw it as a small perk of the job.

But it was something that almost got me into a lot of trouble with the police. It came at a time when Doreen and I didn't have a lot of money. So I thought I would bring home just a few bits of cutlery. One night, after a performance, I intended to take one or two items but ended up with a carrier bag full of this luxurious cutlery. I had an Austin 1100 at the time which I would always park near the Playboy—a little different to the more upmarket cars that used to arrive at the club. But when I left the Playboy that night, I found someone had stolen my car.

I didn't know what to do and I readily admit that I panicked for a while. I had no choice but to go to the local police station in Savile Row armed with this bag full of posh cutlery with knives and forks poking out. Rather than being the victim, I felt like a criminal and as soon as I left the police station, I just emptied the bag in a phone box nearby and ran off. I found my car in a cul-de-sac near to the club, minus a battery. In the days of no mobile phones, I had no choice but to sit in my car and wait for a garage to open. I think I eventually got home after that night's performance at about 10am the next morning.

Aside from such dramas, I had no choice but to combine some good club singing with manual work during the day. At one time, things got so desperate that I would join a long line of cheap labour in Old Kent Road who would just be sent to wherever there might be some work available at the drop of a hat. Another time, I cleaned cars in Forest Gate just to pay the bills.

At least I was still getting bookings so I was able to do the one thing I enjoyed the most. I was appearing in cabaret in glamorous places like the Pigalle and the Blue Angel and also on the famous Bailey circuit in the north of England. I also got a set performing at a lavish evening at the Savoy in front of the Grade family, Bernard Delfonte and Lord Mountbatten. It was a very big deal and I felt something of a fool arriving in my battered Morris Oxford which I paid just £75 for and resembled a hearse. Things took a turn for the worse when I couldn't find anywhere to park it. Running a bit late, I had no choice but to plonk it slap bang in the entrance of the Savoy. To my surprise, and his eternal good manners, the doorman didn't say a word despite the grand occasion. What made me laugh is that years later, I was asked to perform at the opening of a cabaret club in a small Suffolk town. I was playing with a band called Thumper and we borrowed an old transit to carry all our equipment. We tried to park it outside the newly opened building but were told in no uncertain terms that we had to move it straight away. It seems a club in a market town had different rules to a world renowned hotel.

I was at a stage where I was more than happy to branch into different avenues and on one such occasion, I was asked to audition for the West End production of Showboat which would star Cleo Laine in the Adelphi Theatre. It was only a small role but one that interested me greatly. It was something different and who knew where it would take my career? After my initial audition, I was asked back on two occasions and was then offered a part. This whole thing had come a little out of the blue but I was really delighted to be able to have a chance to showcase a different side of me. Only I never got this chance as my manager advised me to turn down the role as he had got me a show in Belfast instead. I was disappointed but went with his advice and the £100 I got from going to Northern Ireland certainly came in handy.

But I don't look back at everything with fondness. That was certainly the case with my stint at the Boulogne in Gerard Street. I was booked for a month but I knew straight away that it wasn't my scene at all. I tried to push this feeling to the back of my mind and dutifully do what I was told by the owners. Initially it went well but as the nights passed, I wasn't clicking with the audience. I would sing songs like Frank Sinatra's Love's Been Good To Me and Resurrection Shuffle but I just didn't feel comfortable and I think that transmitted itself to the customers.

The club was very much like your typical Las Vegas nightspot with girls dancing around in feathers and the like. I can remember one beautiful Indian girl who was there and she was very popular. They wanted her to welcome me onto the stage and she snarled: "He's no f****** star, I'm not going to introduce him." I was shocked of course, but I was even angrier as I felt I should have had more support from people around me. It was made worse by the fact that they never said anything to her when in all fairness, she probably should have been sacked. I was later told she had a problem with me simply because I was black.

It showed that my colour was still an issue for some people even if it wasn't always nasty comments. Sometimes it was just because of what I chose to wear on any given day. My favourite colour was always black and I used to wear a lot of black clothes, both when performing and just day-to-day living. But this had nothing to do with the "black power" that was dominating the headlines, it was simply a personal preference. I had got a booking in Torquay and decided to drive down through the night. When I felt myself getting tired, I stopped off at a little restaurant and ordered a black coffee to perk myself up. The look I got from the waitress was as if I had sworn or something. It was priceless that she was stunned by a black man in black clothing ordering a black coffee. I am sure she thought I was some kind of militant. It seems impossible to imagine now but that is what it used to be like.

Another strange one was when I was shopping in Carnaby Street in the 1980s. At the time, velvet jackets were all the rage and I was wearing a really smart black one. To say it was some kind of political statement, or indeed a fashion one, was just plain ludicrous. But still I had one man approach me in a shop and say to me loud and proud 'black power'. I think he was trying to relate to me, but he would have had a better job if he talked to me about clothes, music or even the weather. I just thought he was a fool.

Race was always an issue though. Someone actually once said to me that the only reason I married a white girl was to try and help me become successful. It was the most ridiculous thing I had ever heard. If that was the case, then I would have woken up every morning next to a white girl in a loveless marriage and screamed.

That sort of thing happened all the time in an industry where jealously was never far away. It might not always have been about colour, but people were quick to try and knock others down if they thought it would help them. Likewise, they would soon jump on your bandwagon if they thought they could make a quick buck out of you.

When I was with The Wranglers and we were in the papers a lot, I didn't have to look hard to find people who would call themselves friends. But when work dried up a little in the 1970s or when I had personal problems, those very same people were nowhere to be seen. Of course it was nice to be approached by producers and other music men when you were successful, it was a good sign that you were doing something right. But you had to quickly learn, and remember, that they were simply looking to cream money for themselves. The biggest problem was when I was let down by people I actually thought were my friends. I think this is one reason why I became an even more insular person who struggled to trust people.

The incident in the Boulogne was typical of my time there and one reason why I just didn't enjoy it. I actually ended up staying there for months, mainly because we needed the cash, but I was fed up. I was honest with the owners and told them I wanted to leave but they always managed to persuade me to stay. I was drawing the punters in, not that you would know it from the posters which showcased the girl dancers but never once showed my face. I can understand that in part, but it still grated with me.

Then one night I was approached by a smartly dressed man who offered to manage me and pay me considerably more than I was getting at the Boulogne. I knew he had put money into a club started by Danny Le Rue so I thought he must know the business a little. When he suggested meeting at the grand Royal Huntingdon Club, I knew he was serious. Doreen and I both went and it seemed that everything was golden. Not used to such lavish surroundings, it didn't impress me. In fact, it frightened the hell out of me. I just wanted someone to get me out so I agreed to sign with him. But when the owner of the Burlogne found out, all hell broke loose.

To make matters worse, it didn't work at all under my new manager. I was just going from one disaster to another. But there was something even more sinister awaiting me.

Chapter Ten: Losing My Mind

Hindsight is such a wonderful thing. In 1970, I suffered a mental breakdown. There were warning signs but only other people spotted them. I was oblivious to where I was heading.

If I had to identify two tipping points In me losing the plot I would say joining a psychedelic rock band called The Cats Pyjamas and the effects of me cheating on Doreen.

Of course, the constant pressure of trying to become a successful performer had taken its toll, as had the putdowns and the remarks that I had tried so desperately to ignore, but which had become ingrained in my mind.

I found going solo quite a daunting experience as I enjoyed having a band on stage with me. Unbeknown to me at the time, The Wranglers had become something of a musical comfort blanket.

Even while I was trying to make it as a solo artist, the need to be in a band continued to gnaw away. One night I was with Peter Gage, who had previously tried to get me in the Ram Jam Band, and his bass player at the Scotch Club in St James when I heard about a band that needed a singer. The band were called the Cats Pyjamas and I can honestly say that joining them was one of my biggest musical mistakes. It was early 1970s and they were into Cream and Eric Clapton as so many people were at the time. I honestly believe the drummer thought he was actually Ginger Baker. It was the time of flower power and most of the band members embraced it. Unfortunately for me, that was the polar opposite of what I was about. We recorded the Ronettes hit Baby I Love You but it didn't do too well. We also did House for Sale which I later recorded a second time when I was living in Thetford.

It was with the Cats Pyjamas that I first stepped foot inside the Bag O'Nails music venue in Kingly Street, Soho. This was a well-known meeting place for musicians in the 1960s, boasting an early gig by the Jimi Hendrix Experience of all people. The band had got signed up with the Rick Gunnell Agency who got us into the club. Playing there was pretty much the only highlight of my time with them though.

I stayed for about a year but I never really fitted in. It wasn't just our musical tastes that differed, I never really clicked with the other band members. I don't think there were any tears shed on either side when we finally decided to part company.

Before that happened, we did manage to secure a month's work in Madrid. A club owner in Spain had heard our version of Baby I Love You and liked it so much that he offered us a month's work performing at his club in the Spanish capital.

There was just one problem—I had only just got married to Doreen. And when I say only just got married I mean literally a week before we were due to be out there. Our wedding was a pretty simple church affair with the reception back at our home. I can remember a couple of youths walking past the church making some snide and racist comment about a black man marrying a white woman but we were past all that by now. We were engaged for quite a few years and to be honest, the thought of marriage never really occurred to me. But this was more to do with the fact that, to me, we had been acting like we were married long before we officially did the deed.

Even though telling your new wife that you needed to go away for a month wasn't the ideal wedding gift, I knew Doreen would be ok. She knew what my singing meant to me and anyway, we needed the money. So our honeymoon period was actually spent apart, with me joined by a group of band members who I didn't really get on with. We performed solely in the one club in Madrid alongside some Italian bands who, in keeping with the whole experience, we clashed with. That said, it wasn't all bad and I actually had quite a good time in what was my first ever trip abroad since moving to England.

There was an American military base nearby and the servicemen would come in and see us and of course they knew all the music we were playing. The most popular cover song we did was Hush by ACDC. I can remember worrying that no one would understand what I was saying but we were treated very well and were actually invited to stay for an extra month. This would have worked out perfectly as Doreen had planned to join us for the extended stay. Unfortunately, Rick told us he had secured more bookings in the UK so we were forced to come back.

When we came back to England, the friction in the band got even worse. We just couldn't get on at all. I started getting angry and answering back, prompting the other guys in the band to claim that I was the one with an attitude problem. The whole situation was very unsavoury and unsurprisingly I had enough. After splitting, I tried to form another band but it didn't work out so I just went out on my own.

I don't blame the band members for my breakdown though. I just should never have joined the band. It was while I was with the group that I cheated on Doreen. I once again sang at the Playboy Club for about a month. While I didn't like the music we were singing, I did enjoy working at the club. We were treated well, with dinner at posh tables and our own changing rooms and Bunny Girls everywhere you look. In addition to our staging area, there were big dance areas, tables and chairs on the outer area and a casino upstairs. I never gambled, I could never afford to even if I wanted to. I remember one man, a banjo player, who would always keep getting re-booked. I couldn't understand it at the time as, I have to admit, I thought I was a lot more talented but found getting more bookings at the Playboy quite tough. But I eventually found out the reason—the man would finish his set, head straight upstairs and spend the money he had just earned on the roulette table. I'm sure he would win on occasions but more often that not, he would just be giving the owners of the Playboy back the money they had paid out only an hour before.

The waitresses would always be walking around, flirting, in a bid to attract the men. I would get a few stars, who shall remain nameless, who would come in and ask me to get the number of a certain girl or two The problem was I wasn't oblivious to the girls either.

What happened next was my single biggest regret in my entire life. Forget my various brushes with fame, cheating on Doreen was the worst thing I have ever done and it will always be something I deeply regret.

How it came about just makes it even more regretful. When I was performing in all these top London clubs, it was a pretty common occurrence to have all these pretty girls come up to you. They would talk to you and flirt with you and basically make it clear what was being offered. I couldn't tell whether they liked me or just liked the fact that I had some success. It is not uncommon, I imagine, to the attention footballers and other celebrities have to put up with. In my experience, there are some women out there who are only interested in what you do for a living.

I was working in the Boulogne in Soho at the time and I had become popular with some of the clientele. I was surrounded by all these pretty girls at the club, but I never chased them. They used to shake me by the hand and give me their card at the same time.

The problem was this often led to a fair degree of jealously among the acts. Perhaps because I was softly spoken or because I was quite into my fashion, some people would call me a 'poof' and things like that. Stupid stuff really, but I think one of the reasons why I slept with someone else was to prove that I wasn't gay. Now it was me who was the stupid one. Just the thought of what I did still makes me cringe. It is something I will regret to my dying day.

I don't deserve any sympathy but from the moment it happened, it effected me profoundly. It eventually led to my breakdown and if I could turn the clock back, I would do so in an instant. But you can't. You just have to live with the consequences of your decisions and try and learn from your mistakes. I was honest with Doreen and though it was understandably difficult to get over, she did forgive me, probably for the kids as much as our marriage. And in time, we were able to move on and become strong once more. For that, I will always be eternally grateful to my beautiful wife.

As well as the pain and suffering I had caused Doreen, the one night stand made me feel really ill. Certain people in the industry knew that I wasn't right in the head and would use it against me.

It all started coming to a head when I was sent to Birmingham for a performance. When I got there, I started feeling really unwell. I know now that I was heading for a breakdown. I was talking nonsense and Doreen kept saying to me that I needed a holiday as I 'wasn't right'. I didn't know it at the time, but she was right. I went to Birmingham on my own, but when I arrived at the club I had to always go through the back door rather than face the public as I was shaking with nerves. I used to be nervous before every performance but this was uncharacteristic stage-fright. I didn't sleep at all for a week and I became very ill.

When I came back, I was asked to be the star of the show at the Celebrity club. It was then that I cracked up. I had a breakdown in the club and everyone just assumed I was on drugs.

The ironic thing is I had never touched drugs in all my time working in London. Of course, it was fairly common but it wasn't for me. I never even smoked a cigarette. Most people didn't seem too bothered whether I took any or not. The only time that I was offered some drugs was after a performance in Madrid. I was called every name under the sun just for turning it down.

As for drink, I could take it or leave it to be honest. Only once did I drink between performances during an interval. I had two glasses of whiskey and it went straight to my head. I came out on stage for the second performance and I didn't even know where I was. I was feeling pretty ill but somehow kept going. When I walked off, I was a pretty sorry sight but the owner seemed really pleased with the set. I couldn't believe it. I quickly made my excuses and slumped off to the dressing room where I stayed for about an hour. Doreen, her brother and his wife were sitting outside waiting for me but I could barely move through a mixture of panic, relief and of course feeling more than a little peculiar. I vowed never to drink again before performing and it is something I have stuck to ever since.

I just allowed everything to build up and my infidelity was the last straw. I just went crazy and didn't know what was happening. I cracked up, shouting and was taken to hospital. The psychiatrist saw me and his immediate diagnosis was spot on. He told Doreen that I looked like the kind of guy who didn't talk much and kept too much in. He had sussed me out straight away. That was my problem and it had finally become my downfall.

My Mum and Dad never pushed me into performing, they just let me to get on with it. They knew music was in my blood. I think the only time they ever worried about the life I was leading was when I had my breakdown.

As is often the case in such circumstances, I didn't know I was suffering mentally or psychologically, let alone that it was the onset of a breakdown. But Doreen knew. She knew me too well and could tell something wasn't right with me. She kept telling me I needed a rest and a holiday, but I wouldn't listen—I just wanted to keep on working. I was obsessed and I don't really know why. I was getting paid for performing, but it was not as if I was earning millions and felt compelled to keep going. In fact, I was getting paid peanuts even though I was the one bringing in the crowds. I was just never one for taking a break and in the end this was my downfall.

The signs were there and it wasn't just Doreen who was spotting them. I was saying some crazy stuff about Frank Sinatra and Nat King Cole having no talent and Louis Armstrong being a load of rubbish. Can you imagine it? A boy from Trinidad criticising these musical greats who were have always been my heroes, and still are to this day. At the time, I hated everybody and everything but it was not me.

The people who didn't really know me thought I was arrogant and knew nothing about music, and I couldn't blame them.

Of course, Doreen was right. My body and mind were crying out for a break. Since I left school in 1957 right up to the 1970, I had never even taken one holiday. I had always been known for having a beaming ear-to-ear smile, but now that had faded and gone.

I remained in hospital for two weeks where I was simply ordered to rest. It was the perfect remedy for me. I played some tennis, relaxed and slept better than I had for a long time. I missed performing but knew it had contributed heavily to my breakdown.

After I was released, I finally took that holiday. We went to Cornwall and it was just the most perfect time surrounded by beautiful beaches. I was finally able to relax for a whole two weeks.

After the holiday, I predictably went straight back to work. I went back to the Celebrity as I felt I was fine, but in hindsight I was still not a well man. People were still putting me down and I soon realised that I had gone back too soon.

Within a year of the breakdown, something far more frightening took place. Doreen gave birth to our first child, Dean.

It was the scariest moment of my life but one of the most wonderful. The fact Doreen was pregnant was one of the reasons why I didn't just walk out of the Celebrity straight away. I had no idea how we would manage without the money I was bringing in with the club. But the first moment I clapped eyes on Dean, I knew all the hardships had been worthwhile. I just couldn't believe he was here, I cried my eyes out to be honest.

With Marsha, our second child, I think we found the experience a little easier as we knew what to expect. She was actually born at home, once we had moved to Thetford, and I waited with Dean downstairs while the midwife looked after Doreen.

As soon as I heard my baby girl's first noise, I rushed upstairs and saw this beautiful sight. Once again I couldn't stop the tears flowing.

Having kids helped me grow up and made me realise what is important in life. I think it was just one more reason why I knew we needed a change. At the same time, they kept me young and allowed me to live my life all over again with them. I thank them both for that.

As I recovered from the breakdown, I realised that I didn't want to perform at the West End anymore. It was that lifestyle, and the personalities around it, that had heavily contributed to my mental problems. The incessant pressure, combined with the far from savoury characters, had finally got to me. On the outside, I was this bubbly character from the Caribbean, but inside I could take no more.

Doreen and I decided to turn our back on London and move to Thetford in Norfolk. It was a bit of a culture shock but the change of pace suited both of us. There were some people in London who wouldn't employ me because they thought Norfolk was too far away, as if I had moved to the moon or something. That was a little annoying but I had to get away from the bright lights of the capital. I knew it had contributed to my breakdown and who knows what would have happened if I had remained right in the heart of all the clubs and big personalities. I wanted to get away. If I hadn't, I probably wouldn't be around today.

The one positive that came out of my breakdown was that I learnt from such an awful experience. I still learn about life even today, at 67 years old, but that experience, one of the worst in my life, made me wiser.

It also made me see things a whole lot clearer. I started worrying far less about what people thought about me. Throughout my whole life, I have laughed off any racist comments. But now I realise what I did let get to me, inside at least, was the constant negative comments from people involved in the showbusiness world. The sniping that I was no good and that I couldn't sing. I didn't know it at the time, but eventually I think this is what wore me down. I ended up believing it and in the end that is what made me go mad.

But leaving London saw me start only worrying about things I could control or that were really important. Things like my family rather than some stranger whose opinion now meant nothing to me. The whole episode changed my outlook on life and made me a better person. Ok, so I am still too soft but that is part of my personality. But I stopped taking things so personally. If someone doesn't like me or my act, I say 'so what'. I'm not changing now. I like me, my family likes me, I like the way I sing.

It was only when my health improved that I realised people couldn't offend me anymore.

Chapter 11: Touring With Dionne Warwick

Some people thought I had made it. That the reason we had decided to leave London for Norfolk was because we had a lot of money and could afford to enjoy the trappings of the countryside.

They were unaware of my breakdown and why would they know? It was an intensely personal matter for me and my family. It was 1973 when we decided to move out of the capital. Doreen was always telling me we needed to leave and that the stress would prove too much.

As always, her wisdom was spot on. I had tried to get over the breakdown by remaining in London and trying to get my life back to normal by playing in the West End. But it didn't take long before I too realised it was time to take something of a step back.

We had visited Norfolk before as we had friends living in the town. We moved as part of the London overspill and we were offered a house on the Abbey Farm estate. Nowadays, this area has something of a bad name, an underserved one in my opinion. But moving there from Forest Gate, the estate was like something I had never seen before. There were all these trees around and the river and it didn't take me long to forget all about the high life in London.

Doreen got a job in the offices of the Jeyes Group, where they manufacture hygiene products, almost straight away and I became a welder for a local company where I stayed for about 10 years. To this day, I still don't really know how to weld but it paid the bills. I returned to London at weekends to play but I found this more manageable. I never yearned to return to the capital permanently, it was nice coming back to Norfolk where I now classed as home.

After the initial culture shock as I adapted to the slowness of life in the countryside, we soon settled and we even managed to visit my parents who by this time had returned to live in Trinidad, before finally returning to England to be closer to their grandchildren.

While the chances offered to me were becoming few and far between, that doesn't mean they never came. It had been almost 10 years since I had met Dionne Warwick while fronting The Wranglers. She had wanted us to go on tour with her and when we sadly declined her tempting offer, she promised it would happen one day. Naturally, I had pretty much forgotten about this conversation.

But one day, while I was still working as a welder, I got a call out of the blue asking if I would like to open for Ms Warwick. These chances don't come along very often so I naturally jumped at it. I played a few nights in Birmingham and Liverpool. Occasionally the crowd was tough as they wanted Warwick but got Bernard instead. But it was still an experience I looked back on with some fondness.

I didn't speak to Dionne too much. She liked to keep herself to herself and her dressing room was quite private. But on the occasions I did, I found her to be a most pleasant companion and I will always value the fact that she kept her word in an industry where such a trait is a precious commodity. What was funny was that I never even told any of my work colleagues I had toured with Dionne Warwick. I always wanted to keep my singing and my day job separate. So I simply took a week off work and left them oblivious.

Eventually, I also got a job at Jeyes where I ended up working for 18 years. It was here that I really took up singing again. At weekends, I would travel back to London and work at the Celebrity, there was quite a lot of work at the time. I think any chances of me having a hit record had gone and I slowly accepted that. Being away from the heart of the action made it difficult. I was still returning to London to play at weekends but bit by bit, I was edging further out of the West End and more onto the periphery.

It meant I wasn't mixing with the same club owners that dominated the West End. To them, my decision to move to Thetford probably spoke volumes about my own heart not being in it anymore. I didn't mind though. I could just concentrate on what I enjoyed the most and that is performing.

My music dream had all but died and we still needed to pay the bills. I worked in the factory at nights and weekends to earn more money. All I had to do was put boxes onto palettes so it wasn't the most exciting employment but it paid the mortgage and Doreen and I were happy.

Working in the factory was of course worlds away from being in the West End. But there were advantages to that as well. I worked with good people and a good company, something I wasn't always used to in London. Some people at Jeyes had seen my film and tried to convince me that I take singing more seriously again. But my confidence was low, to be honest it had been virtually shattered from my experiences in London. I was happy to perform a few nights here and there but even that was starting to dwindle a little.

Certain people had broken my love of singing, it had got that bad. I was pretty depressed with the way parts of my life had turned out. I had beautiful children and loved my wife very much, but I was no longer singing and in a job that I really didn't like. Getting up every day for work had become a chore and I was at a pretty low ebb. I wanted to leave but it was only when I was diagnosed with an eye problem that I was forced to retire. It is a funny thing to say but it turned out to be a Godsend. It got me out of the rigmarole of working in a factory day after day.

I only have good things to say about Jeyes. I enjoyed my time there, they treated Doreen fantastically well and my daughter still works there in the accounts department. It has been a good company for my family and I remain in contact with people who work there. When I was working there, they would tell me that I had a talent and should go out and flaunt it. Following all the problems and criticism I received from certain people in London, that kind of encouragement meant a lot and I will never forget it.

It was while living in Thetford that Doreen and I became good friends with the West Indian cricketer Ian Bishop and his lovely wife Jan. I had actually first got to know Ian through my sister, Barbara, who was best friends with his future wife. Jan would occasionally stay with my family and, after she had met Ian, she actually stayed with Doreen and I for a month. She wanted to be a nurse and had applied for a job at the West Suffolk Hospital in Bury St Edmunds. At that time, Ian had left the West Indies and was playing for Derbyshire Cricket Club. This was before he was married and Ian asked if I could visit him and keep him company as he was a bit lonely at a new club in a new country. My son Dean and I went up there a couple of times to keep him company and watch some cricket.

Occasionally Jan would stay with us in Thetford as she and Doreen became quite close and Ian would also take the spare room whenever Derbyshire played Essex at Chelmsford. What struck me straight away about Ian was how kind he was, with no airs and graces from such a successful playing career. To say thank you for our hospitality, he would always leave tickets for us at the gate which meant I got to see first hand what an impressive cricketer he was. When I used to see him bowl, I just couldn't believe that any batsman could actually see the ball—it was a blur to me from my position in the stands.

Ian and Jan got married in Trinidad and we have always stayed in touch. Jan would always make a point of calling us on our anniversary and even to this day, Ian and I meet up whenever he is in England. It is clear how much Doreen meant to Jan. She used to say how she would never forget how we looked after her when she was first courting Ian. The last time we visited Trinidad before Doreen died, we stayed with them and we always had a good time in their company. Ian is a good person and people would always come up to him in Trinidad and ask for his autograph. He always had time for everyone, even though he is actually quite shy in private. You would never know this by how he comes across on television.

Not having a day job, I found myself becoming refocused towards music. I was writing a little, working a lot and my enthusiasm for entertainment slowly returned. It was perhaps no coincidence that at the same time, I was introduced to the song Big Panty Woman.

I had just finished a gig in a village near Thetford called Mundford when I was approached by a man offering me a song. This had happened a lot when I was singing in London but it was a lot rarer now I was playing away from the capital. He gave me a cassette of a song he had heard while out in Kenya. I was intrigued and as soon as I got home, I put it in the cassette player. I liked it straight away, it had a nice rhythm and I thought it would suit my voice. The fact that it was about ladies with larger derrieres made me laugh and I instantly thought we could have some fun with such a vibrant song.

I started singing it wherever I performed and over the years I noticed that it was becoming more and more popular. No one had ever heard Big Panty Woman before but it proved that a catchy number will get people dancing and smiling. On one occasion, some perhaps inebriated women had come out of the toilet with underwear over their trousers. It was some sight but just added to the sense of fun centred around the song. How could I not get my love of music back when greeted with such sights?

But it wasn't all about large ladies undergarments and pleasing the crowds. In April 2003, my Mum passed away. Perhaps what was most fitting is that a local newspaper in Trinidad did a glowing obituary on her. It was written by a journalist called Angela Pidduck who had become a good friend of my Mum's after she had been taught by her from the age of four.

The article in Trinidad newspaper Newsday, dated April 20, 2003 included a beautiful photo of my Mum from her youth and read:

A NEWSPAPER colleague once said to me 'you know Ange, younger women nowadays think they know about women's lib, but it's really you older women who started the ball rolling, and at that, in times when women just didn't do certain things'.
The death of Mildred Pinder-Bernard last week in England brought that remark strongly to mind.
"Teacher Mildred", as I called her from the time she taught me at age four to spell 'cat, bat and rat' up to the day of her passing at age 82, was my second teacher. The first, my maternal grandmother Emmeline Gabrielle Superville, a former government school principal, had

already taught me the alphabet, numbers, colours and shapes.

Mildred Pinder was born in Poole, south Trinidad. She came to live in Greenhill Village, where her father was the District Warden, as a very young woman and ran the village post office which was located next to her parents' home. "Millie", as my mother always called her, taught the Aches and Days (about six of us) in an alcove at the back of the post office counter while handing out mail and selling her stamps.

There was never anything laidback about this lady. Even her choice of suitor and future husband, Clive Bernard, added some excitement to the sleepy village as he roared down the one main road to visit here on his motorcycle. The braver of us children would accept a ride now and then. Her marriage to Clive provided a lifelong family joke, as my sister was a flower girl and, to appease me, Teacher Mildred said that I would be a 'guest'. Of course, not fully understanding that every other person in the wedding was a guest, I boasted to all and sundry about it until full realisation hit years later.

Clive and Millie had three children, a son Kenneth and twins Barbara and Ansel, by which time the family moved to San Fernando and she became a hairdresser. In no time at all, this very progressive woman realised that rearing three children on a small income was not cutting it for her family and persuaded her more laidback husband that migration was the way to go. The Bernards sailed off to England leaving family and good friends behind.

After many years in England where she was a first-class hair stylist, their children now grown, the couple returned to Trinidad and bought a home in

Marli Street, Newtown. For Millie, there was more yet to be done in her life and she purchased a small guest house at Black Rock, Tobago, which with Clive's help, became like a home away from home for her visitors.

At an age when most people would stay put, Millie decided it was time to return to England where their older son still lived.

But retirement was not about sitting in a rocking chair beside an English fireplace, the Bernards moved between their homes in Trinidad, Orlando (Florida) and England Millie's beloved Clive passed away about five years ago. Teacher Mildred, whose hearty laugh, pleasant manner and loving and caring ways I will never forget, succumbed to a stroke on Friday April 4.

Her funeral service took place last Tuesday, followed by a cremation.

A beautiful eulogy and one that still gets me choked up eight years after it was written.

Chapter 12: Northern Soul

I have to be honest and say I knew very little about Northern Soul. I didn't know what was classed as this type of music, who sung it and who liked it. So imagine my surprise when I was told that I had become something of a cult hit within the genre.

It all started with my song What Love Brings. When we moved to Norfolk, I had pretty much left the business behind. My breakdown had soured my hopes of making it and I was content enough to move to Thetford with Doreen and settle into a normal job with a bit of performing on the side.

I was working as a welder when it all started. I came home one day and Doreen said I had received a call from someone at Pye Records. Now this was something of a surprise given the way I had left the business and the fact that I had gone missing in action for quite some time.

Pye was still a big player at that time with some big stars signed up. Best of all, they had told Doreen that one of my songs had taken off, even if they had refused to tell her which one. I instantly thought it was some kind of joke. But when I dared to believe that it might be true, I assumed it was going to be Ain't No Soul Left In These Old Shoes.

They called back and to my surprise I learnt that What Love Brings had finally taken off. The first song I had done as a solo artist had not really taken off at the time. Now here was some stranger telling me on the end of a phone that a song I had pretty much forgotten about was suddenly popular with something called the Northern Soul circuit. I thought some of my other songs were more soul-orientated but, as I say, I knew very little about this phenomenon.

It transpired that Pye Records had been trying to track me down for the last month, but had no idea that I had moved out of the city. Of course when I had the breakdown and we decided to move away from London, we did so very quietly. It was no one else's business, no one else's concern. I just wanted a new start and to leave my old life behind. Now I was hearing that this might not be so easy to do, but of course I was very interested in finding out more about this supposed success.

The chap from Pye said they eventually tracked me down at my old address in Forest Gate where they were given my new phone number by a neighbour—they were certainly keen to speak to me. To my astonishment, I was told that What Love Brings had been popular for years among the kids, who would think nothing of forking out quite a bit of money for a rare copy. They liked what they heard and they didn't mind paying a bit extra for it.

As I say I didn't know much about the Northern Soul circuit, but I quickly learnt. I was told there was a casino in Wigan which acted as a focal point for the music. They made arrangements for me to go to the casino and when I arrived, I had never seen anything like it. I had walked into this massive hall and it was jam-packed, you couldn't move. Everyone was going crazy and as soon as I walked through the door people were coming up to me and asking if I was Kenny Bernard.

The adulation was intense, even more so than when the Wranglers were at our peak. These people had my records and they couldn't believe they were seeing me in the flesh. It was a little strange but very, very flattering. Pye had fixed it for me just to sing one song so I did What Love Brings and everyone went crazy. They also told me they liked Pity My Feet which I couldn't even remember recording. It was like a special guest appearance but I had no idea it was going to be anything like this.

I hadn't realised it at the time but the Wigan Casino was a real big deal for northern soul music attracting the likes of Jackie Wilson and Edwin Starr.

Young people from all over the UK would go there and happily queue around the block to hear the latest northern soul artists and I was later told that What Love Brings had become big because of massive exposure in the discos in the north.

The Casino was once voted the best disco in the world by American music magazine Billboard and even today, it remains one of the most famous clubs in the North of England.

In the end, Pye decided to release What Love Brings to try and tap into this new-found success. But once again the single came out without any real backing so when it didn't do very well, they could be comforted by the fact that they didn't lose any money on it. But with that kind of minimal support, there was little chance of it ever being a success. It was a joke really.

Here I was, having never heard of Northern Soul or Wigan Casino, but suddenly becoming something of a cult hit. It was a truly amazing feeling when I walked into the casino the first time and I must thank everyone who was there for the reception they gave me. I have had some tough times and lowlights in the industry, but that was sure up there as one of the better moments.

A few years later, I got invited back and this time sung Pity My Feet. The reaction in this massive auditorium was exactly the same. More hysteria, more photos, more people wanting to kiss and hug me. I did a 45-minute Northern Soul show in Northampton and took Doreen with me. We stayed over and the next morning when I came down for breakfast, the star treatment continued. They waited on us hand and foot and nothing was too much trouble.

Ain't No Soul Left In These Old Shoes eventually became a Northern Soul favourite after it had been on the B side of Hey Woman. I of course had high hopes for the A track becoming a massive hit but I still took great pride in the success of Ain't No Soul.

I have also done Northern Soul nights in Blackpool and Hunstanton and they have always been sell outs. Now this is obviously not just because of me but it shows how popular the genre of music is. And my small part in the event has always gone down really well with people asking for more and me always obliging with encores.

To this day, I am still not sure if I am a true Northern Soul singer. I have always just enjoyed singing and hoped that people would like what I produce. People have said to me in the past that I should just concentrate on the Northern Soul stuff and try and make money from that. But while I am grateful for all the kind words and support I have received, I have always enjoyed singing different stuff to different people.

It was amazing although a little surreal as to the vast majority of people in the music business, I had become a nobody. I have to admit it was nice receiving that support again, even if it was only for a short time. I had missed it and to feel like a star again was pretty special.

Chapter 13: You Came Into My Life

I knew something was seriously wrong. For a few years, Doreen kept getting acid in her throat and was struggling to sleep at nights. It was not long before she was diagnosed with stomach cancer and told she just had a year to live.

It was a bolt out of the blue for me and the family and I struggled at first. I didn't know what I was going to do without my wife of more than 40 years. We had a little bit of money at the time so I sought advice from specialists in London and Liverpool but they all told me there was nothing they could do.

Typically, Doreen was a lot stronger and braver than me. She never cried in front of me, not even when I got upset or a member of her family was crying on the end of the phone.

She started chemotherapy but the doctors soon had to stop this because she was diabetic so it was damaging her kidneys. There was nothing more they could do. In the year before she died, Doreen barely ate a thing. I would often have to force a few spoonfuls of soup into her mouth but that was about it. It was heartbreaking to watch but even then, she retained her grace and I was very proud of her for that.

In the weeks before she died, she started attending St Nicholas Hospice Care in Bury St Edmunds. She would go to Orchard Day Therapy which would give her the chance to talk to nurses as well as other cancer patients. I know it was something she benefitted from and it gave her the chance to get away from me for a day. It also meant that I had some respite from my role as Doreen's primary carer. Eventually, we had community nurses come to the house as well before Doreen was admitted to West Suffolk Hospital for the last couple of weeks of her life.

Throughout all her pain and suffering, Doreen did receive such wonderful care from every doctor and nurse who treated her. The hospital kept trying to make her last few days as comfortable as possible, even though the nurses would occasionally get cross with Doreen for not asking for help. It was just not her way, she didn't want to be any trouble to anyone.

The hospital and the hospice were nothing but a source of comfort to her and our whole family appreciated everything that was done.

I wanted to raise money for the Hospice to thank them for everything they did and for all the staff and volunteers there who were exceptionally good. I held gigs at a number of pubs and clubs in the local area after she died and there were also lots of donations to the hospice. Everyone was so generous, especially Jeyes where Doreen worked for so many years. She was held in high esteem there and they raised £600 for the Hospice just through a whip-round among staff. People even stopped me in the street just to give me money for the charity. People in Thetford and beyond were very supportive in what was an incredibly difficult time.

Doreen and I met at primary school age and were together for more than 40 years. We had survived fractious racial relations, my depression and the problems that being in the music business can bring She was my rock.

Doreen was a lovely and special woman who stood by me through so much. I loved the fact that she was never that impressed by the music scene in London during the 1960s. She could certainly take or leave all the nightlife, the dancing girls and the big names. I once took her to see James Brown but she wasn't that impressed. She was more a Johnny Mathis or Nat King Cole girl. As she grew older, she also liked The Stylisticts. I think that is one reason why we stayed together for so long. Whether music produced good times or bad, she never changed towards me.

We could have easily been divided by colour or at least the comments and the issues that other people had. But we rarely spoke about it. When she became ill, she once told me that she had always thought we were different, even though it didn't matter to her. But I told her that I never saw any difference, she was just my Doreen and her colour never came into it.

Doreen was a fantastic wife and it was not until she passed away that I realised how lucky I was. I don't think I appreciated her enough when she was alive. Through all the ups and downs, the late nights and the long hours, she was brilliant. She would always try and lift my spirits and would always be supportive of my music. I have a good friend who helps me with my equipment when I perform. But one night, a few months before Doreen passed away, he couldn't make a particular show. I was working in Cambridge in a local pub and just decided to carry everything and set up on my own. As I was doing this, suddenly Doreen walked into the pub. Putting aside her own illness, she had driven on her own to make sure I was alright and could manage. That was the kind of woman Doreen was.

No one ever had a bad word to say about Doreen. We had friends who phoned every day after they heard Doreen had cancer. We had also made friends with a couple from Indiana when we visited America. One of them, the son of the couple we had become friendly with, lost his job at Chrysler shortly after Doreen passed away. I can remember one night I was sitting in my chair when I heard a knock at the front door. To my surprise, there stood Francis who had just decided to fly all the way from America to make sure I was ok. I was shocked but so touched and it just showed me how much Doreen meant to people. Francis ended up staying with me for about four days at a time when I really needed company. It was a gesture that I will never forget nor be able to repay. It meant everything to me and showed me he was a real friend. Plus he had his first ever English breakfast so he was happy.

It was a source of comfort to me but I was still alone, frightened and without my soul mate. Everyday I think it is unfair what happened to Doreen and some days it is difficult getting out of bed. My family have always been there to keep me going, my beautiful children and my adventurous, sweet and soulful grandchildren.

I love being a granddad. With Doreen not here, it helps when they turn up. The little one, Kyran, is going to be like me. He's six years old but he is already learning chords on the guitar and he is always writing songs. Sometimes when I perform, he comes with me and even starts singing on stage on occasions.

Jaden is the complete opposite to his cousin. He is a lot quieter and more sensitive. But occasionally he comes out with some real corking lines. We were on holiday in Ibiza when he saw a white man get changed on the beach. Next thing I know, bold as brass, he loudly asked me if I had a white bum. They are both great grandchildren and a real credit to their parents.

And then there is music. My attitude to music has changed a little since Doreen passed away. There are some songs I find difficult to perform. Recording Seven Spanish Angels was a very personal project to me. The song had originally been written by Willie Nelson and Ray Charles and talks about how angels will be taken home.

I recorded it just before Doreen died and to this day I still can't sing or even play it. The only exception was when I was asked on two separate occasions to sing it at funerals of friends who had passed away.

The lyrics are particular moving:

"He looked down into her blue eyes, and said 'say a prayer for me'.

She threw her arms around him, whispered 'God will keep us free'.

They could hear the riders coming., he said 'this is my last fight'.

If they take me back to Texas, they won't take me back alive.

There were seven Spanish angels, at the altar of the sun.

They were praying for the lovers, in the valley of the gun.

When the battle stopped and the smoke cleared, there was thunder from the throne.

And seven Spanish angels took another angel home."

I was asked if I wanted to sing the song at Doreen's funeral but I just couldn't. Instead it was played when her coffin was brought into the church and at the end, when I finally broke down. My daughter, Marsha, was a rock to me that day. I used to listen to Bob Harris' country show on the radio when Doreen went to bingo. I liked the show but didn't always relate to the songs he played. Now I find it difficult to even put the station on.

Just months before Doreen was diagnosed with cancer, we decided to write a song together. We had never done anything like this before but one day I was sitting at the table when I started humming a tune. Doreen told me to be quiet because she wanted to watch the television, but I knew I was onto something.

I told her I liked this tune and asked if she wanted to help me put some words to go with it. She was a little shy at first but we decided to write about my life in showbusiness. After I had put a few words down, Doreen took over. She was better with words than me and who else knew more about my life than my wife? When she became ill, we brought up the song, You Came Into My Life, again and I asked Doreen what she wanted to do with it. She was insistent that we got it recorded as she wanted to have it as a keepsake for the grandchildren.

Just a day before she died at just 64 years old, the CD arrived through our letterbox. Although we didn't know it when we started writing, You Came Into My Life was our way of saying goodbye to each other. The song means so much to me, but because it was about our time together, I haven't been able to sing it again since Doreen passed.

It is a wonderful memory of our time together and even if I never play it or sing it again, it will always give me nothing but warm memories of my Doreen.

Chapter 14: Hopes And Dreams

After losing Doreen, I needed something to focus on and music helped.

Since moving to Thetford, I have been lucky enough to meet some great people and play at some great places. To this day, I still have a gig virtually every week in some pub, club or holiday camp across Norfolk, Suffolk and Essex. At a time when the economic pressures have seen many businesses cut their entertainment bill, I know I am fortunate to still be able to make money from my music.

I still record songs, finally getting round to House for Sale after the Cats Pyjamas first sung it. Naturally, it was done a little more to my tastes this time around. I have had my good times and bad times in music but I wouldn't change a thing. I have played gigs to just two people in a pub and I have played at the London Palladium. I have recorded with a big band orchestra and I have performed in a holiday camp when my disco CD player packed up during the middle of the act. But like I have always done, I react to anything and everything with a big smile. When the music stopped, I just started a rendition of Blueberry Hill and everyone joined in.

I will always retain my love of music and performing and you never know what is round the corner. Such was the case when I got a call completely out of the blue from a London-based record label called Acid

Jazz who have connections with Radio 2 DJ Mark Lamarr.

The label said they wanted to meet me in person and invited me to come to their offices in Soho. I was a little sceptical at first—suffering so many knockbacks in the music industry will do that to you. But within a few days, I was travelling to Bethnal Green Road to meet the guys connected with the label, which specialises in releasing little-known albums from the 1960s. I took my son Dean with me as I wanted his take on this. As I say, I was a little more cautious and less foolhardy than I had been in the past.

They explained that they had found what they thought was a live recording of Kenny and the Wranglers performing at the Ad Lib Club in 1965 and they wanted to release it on their label. I'm not a businessman, I have always played from the heart, but they offered me a down-payment there and then. It was the first time in my whole life I had been offered a down-payment. They then said they wanted to put one of The Wranglers' old songs, a cover of Midnight Hour, on a special compilation album entitled Rare Mod Volume 3 which was a collection of 1960s underground rhythm 'n' blues, psych and soul.

The whole thing was pretty crazy and incredible at the same time. I had been out of the spotlight for such a long time and here was someone telling me they wanted to release my album and revisit those wild and crazy days. While I hadn't thought about it in a long time, I can remember the events leading up to that live recording like it was yesterday.

It was in 1965 when I was performing at the Ad Lib club when I recognised Peter Sellars in the audience. He was sitting with a familiar-looking Italian chap whose face I knew from the television. But for the life of me, I could not put a name to the face despite wracking my brains for the whole night. I was later put out my misery when a colleague said it was Vittorio de Sica from The Four Just Men, a television series that ran in the later 1950s and early 1960s.

Perhaps not learning from my interlude with Sammy Davis Jnr, I cracked a joke over the microphone towards Peter's table. But where Sammy Davis had failed to see the funny side, there was no such problems this time and they started laughing. During the interval, I was in the dressing room as usual when someone came in and said Peter Sellars wanted a word with me. This was one of the radio stars from The Goon Show so I felt quite honoured by the invitation. He bought me a gin and tonic and told me how much he was enjoying the show. He also suggested that we should record our performance one evening. The seeds of a great idea had been sown and we went to talk with our managers about setting a live recorded performance into motion.

The first problem was choosing what songs we were going to perform. I wanted to do Shout and Change Is Gonna Come but the bosses at Pye wouldn't let me. Then there was the actual logistics of producing a live performance in a smoky, boisterous London club. In the end, our record company decided to get the band into the studio to perform a live set which would then be overdubbed to give the feel of a live show. We laid down the tracks in August 1965 and a handful of test pressings were made. But for one reason or another, Pye Records decided not to release the album, probably thinking it wouldn't make enough money. Of course a year later Geno Washington and the Ram Jam Band released the legendary Foot Stomping album which sold millions. Had Pye been brave enough to release our 'live' album just 12 months before, we too could have become a household name.

In the recording, we played an instrumental which went on for about six minutes but it sounded really good, but then and to this day. I was told that Mark Lamarr had found a recording in a market and when he played it, he thought it was fantastic. It's funny because one of the songs on it was Shout which of course had been labelled as "jungle music" at the time. Even at the time, we still didn't think we were that good but I have to say listening to the recording now, it sounds good and it brings back so many memories, good and bad. I sang I'll Go Crazy by James Brown and Shout and the Lady is a Tramp.

The experience just shows that you never know how your life is going to turn out. I had largely been out of the industry for 30 years and then the right person buys the right album on a market stall, and things can change.

Just a few months later, 'Kenny Bernard and the Wranglers—Live '65', had hit the shelves.

With eight tracks and a colour sleeve detailing the history of myself and the band, it was fantastic to see the album finally released—and prove very popular too.

Since Doreen's passing, I have always thought that someone was watching out for me.

I have never really been spiritual, but certainly things have happened in the last couple of years that have made me wonder.

I mean, what are the chances of someone like Mark Lamarr finding an old album of mine on a market stall and then releasing it to the world?

I will keep performing until the day I die as it is in my blood. I have had some great nights when people have shouted for an encore. On the flipside, you are always going to get nights that don't go quite so well. On one occasion, I was actually asked to stop after singing just three songs. I went up to the owner and I think he thought I was going to hit him. But I have been in the business too long to get uptight or upset. It was his call and to be fair, he still paid me my full amount. It made me laugh though that I could go down a hit in the Palladium but get paid to leave at a small holiday camp which shall remain nameless.

Every artist has gone through good times and bad. One of the people in music I most admire is Bill Wyman, a man who gives me inspiration to keep performing even though we are not on the same scale. I had first met him in 1963 at St Michael's Hall in Lower Sydenham when he was in the group The Cliftons. He actually mentioned us briefly in his book Stone Alone. Having not seen Bill for 40 years, it was a pretty special moment for me when I met him before his gig at the Cambridge Corn Exchange last year.

I'm told Bill rarely speaks to anyone outside his circle on the day of the gig because he is concentrating on putting on the best show possible. So I was deeply honoured when he gifted me an audience just a few hours before going on stage as part of his national tour. We discussed the old days and our experiences and to be honest I could have reminisced all day. Instead, it was soon time to let Bill prepare but I will always be grateful for the time he gave me.

I never had much interest in making loads of money. All I wanted to do was make good music. Of course, the two often went hand-in-hand. I would have loved to have had a big hit in the Fab 40, as it was known then, and naturally that would have brought with it some degree of fame and fortune.

Whether I would have been able to handle any success is something I have always wondered. Looking back, people will think I was a cross between naïve and stupid and in a way they would be right. But there is a part of me that is glad I never had a hit record and became so successful. With the way the industry was at that time, I might not have been alive today. I certainly don't have any regrets. I think I could have had a hit record but it would have been done in the wrong way.

I feel that too often the people behind me treated me like some kind of football pools. They were only willing to put a shilling on me and hoped that their numbers came up, as if by luck. I'm not saying I wanted, nor expected, thousands of pounds pumped into me, whether as a solo artist or in The Wranglers. But if a relatively sizeable sum had been invested, I am certain I would have had a proper hit. That is not me blowing my own trumpet or anything, I just think the songs I was singing needed a bit of backing as well.

Of course my colour came into it, there is no getting away from that point. People were too scared of trying to promote a black man at that time, especially one fronting a white band. But it wasn't just me who suffered, there were a number of black artists who faced the same problems. For instance, while The Beatles were understandably loved and adored by all, there were many black singers from the Liverpool area who virtually sunk without a trace.

What now wouldn't make anyone blink an eyelid was deemed too much of a risk in the 1960s. It was meant to be all flower power and peace and love, but there were still too many conservative people about it. Unfortunately, in the music business, they were the ones who had all the money and therefore wielded all the influence.

Had I come into the music scene a decade later, it would have been a lot, lot easier. The likes of Stevie Wonder had paved the way and I really believe I would have made it. At any rate, there would have been far less obstacles in my way. It would have come down to my talent rather than my colour. But I wasn't alone. I've heard interviews with Diana Ross saying that she encountered problems even though she, like me, was brought up never to notice colour. Sam Cooke and Ray Charles were others and the things they all had in common was how they turned to entertainment as a way of trying to break down barriers.

I have been described as a pioneer before and while I am not sure if that is true, I just always wanted to entertain people through my music. When you get applause after a good performance, there is no better feeling in the world.

The music industry is also about getting the right breaks and that can often come down to luck. Being in the right time at the right place, that kind of thing. Unfortunately I never had that which was down to many factors including mistakes on my part.

When things weren't going well and I was quite low, Doreen used to tell me to stop performing. She knew how much I loved singing but she hated to see me hurting. But here I am, 66 years old and still going strong, well pretty much.

The words and the feeling of the song have always been the most important thing for me. If I can't connect with it, I would never sing a certain song, even if it might have been a hit. In the past, I sang what I was told to but now I am older, and wiser, I only sing songs that I know are right for me.

I still have ambitions. My dream was always to have a gold disc as I always likened it to winning a gold medal at the Olympics. While I think that it might be a little too late for me to sell 300,000 singles, I do still have hopes and dreams.

I am hoping to perform at the old actors retirement home. Peter Elliott is the man. It might sound strange but I have a hope that I can sing Big Panty Woman with the Roly Polys backing me up. It would certainly be a sight and would sure to raise a smile. After all, isn't that what entertainment is all about?